CHRISTIAN RATIONALISM AND PHILOSOPHICAL ANALYSIS

CHRISTIAN RATIONALISM
AND
PHILOSOPHICAL ANALYSIS

BY

F. H. CLEOBURY
PH.D. (LONDON)

JAMES CLARKE & CO. LTD.
33, Store Street
London, W.C.1

First published 1959

© F. H. Cleobury 1959

PRINTED IN GREAT BRITAIN
BY LATIMER, TREND AND CO. LTD.
PLYMOUTH

FOREWORD

Anyone who at the present time offers a rationalistic exposition and defence of the Christian faith is opposing what has been, so far, one of the main trends of thought in the English-speaking world in the twentieth century. In philosophy there has been a wave of empiricism and positivism, and in theology the tendency has been to disparage any appeal to the reasonableness of religious belief and to concentrate on historical and dogmatic theology—the theology of the Word—of Revelation.

It would be absurd, of course, to dismiss these twentieth-century tendencies as merely mistaken. They have exposed real weaknesses in the older religious rationalism. But, like most reactions, they have gone too far, and it is necessary to insist on the validity of human reasoning in the interpretation of religious experience and in the exposition and defence of the Faith. A scepticism about the validity of our reasoning processes is the most dissolving of all scepticisms. If reasoning cannot be trusted, then the writings of *all* schools are invalidated. But in the very act of showing that reason cannot be trusted you are, in effect, appealing to the validity of the reasoning you declare invalid. And if there were no *reason* for believing in God there would be no reason for believing that any human experience was His revelation.

5

There is not the slightest reason for thinking that man's sinfulness impairs his reasoning processes *as such*, whether deductive or inductive. It may, indeed, prevent his arriving at right *conclusions*, but this is because it vitiates the selection of the data to which he attends. We all tend, subconsciously, to shy away from any facts which would convince us of the truth of what we do not wish to believe. But this is an impairment of the will, not of the intellect.

CONTENTS

7

CONTENTS

1

RECENT PHILOSOPHY AND THE
CHRISTIAN FAITH

When philosophy in the English-speaking world took a new direction under the influence of Russell, Moore and Wittgenstein in the early years of this century it was not long before three trends of argument, all hostile to Christianity, were given great emphasis. First there was the attempt of the logical positivists of the twenties and thirties to dismiss as meaningless all "metaphysical" statements, including statements about God. Second, there came the denial that sentences about right and wrong conduct were statements of fact. If I say "That was a wrong thing to do" I am not, on that view, making a statement which agrees or disagrees with any state of affairs outside the field of human emotions or attitudes, and which therefore can be true or false. I am merely expressing my feelings, as when I say "Oh!", or am taking up an attitude, or am exhorting people to do what I want them to. Third, there came the attempt, known as "logical behaviourism", to equate statements about mental or conscious processes to statements about bodily ones.

These are definite attacks on the Christian faith. Some would deny this, and tell us that the analytical philosopher is merely applying a certain method, with no motive other than the clarification of thought or the resolving of puzzles. But this would be to confuse the ideal with the actual; we are living in an imperfect world. It did not need Freud to tell us that men can be dominated by motives which they do not admit; it did not need the existentialists to tell us that a man's attitude to ultimate questions is not a detached act of pure thought but a commitment of his whole personality. All this was known to the insight of biblical writers.

He would be credulous indeed who would regard it as a pure coincidence that the three trends I have mentioned—which represent quite central and important features of the philosophical landscape of the first half of the twentieth century—have been in effect denials of what Kant saw to be the essence of religious belief—God, moral responsibility and immortality. Language about God had no meaning. Statements about right and wrong revealed nothing but human attitudes, and therefore our moral consciousness could not reveal the will of God and our responsibility to Him. Statements about conscious events like thinking and loving and willing were *really* (i.e. could adequately be translated into) statements about bodily activities and dispositions, and therefore the idea that human personality could survive the death of the body was nonsense. I propose in this section briefly to consider these three trends in turn.

The attack on metaphysics took the form of an assertion that all significant factual sentences (sentences, that is, which are not overtly or covertly exhortations, exclamations, commands, etc.) can be exhaustively divided into two classes: (1) Sentences the truth or falsity of which can be decided by examining their logical form *alone*, without any reference to "facts" or to "the real world". Sentences in this class, if seen to be true, are seen to be *necessarily* true. Examples are the propositions of pure mathematics and pure logic. For example 'If the affirmation of proposition A implies the affirmation of proposition B, then the denial of B implies the denial of A'. (2) Sentences which purport to convey information about happenings in the real world, and which can be verified or falsified by sense-experience or experiment. At the outset it was alleged that since statements about God fell into neither class, they were "metaphysical" and meaningless.

But this short and easy way of disposing of God was soon seen through. Consider the sentence 'Statements which cannot be verified by sense-experience are meaningless'. Is this *necessarily* true? Does your contradiction of it land you in self-contradiction? Clearly not. Is it itself verifiable or falsifiable by sense-experience? Clearly not. It is therefore, on your own showing, meaningless as a statement of fact. The new doctrine, therefore, was seen to be nothing more than a *proposal* to give the word 'meaning' a new and unusual meaning—a proposal to which there is no compelling reason for agreeing. But further doubts about the new doctrine began to emerge. *Can* we avoid "metaphysics" even if we wish to? Does anyone ever, in fact, avoid metaphysical assumptions? J. O. Urmson has pointed out[1] that the early work of Wittgenstein pre-supposed a doctrine of "logical atomism" which was itself a metaphysic; there was no way of verifying it in experience. "But it is clearly undesirable to derive an anti-metaphysical principle from a metaphysical doctrine in this way."

The general tendency of later analysts has been to regard the business of the philosopher as the study of the functions of various types of sentence. What experiences prompt them, and what is our real purpose (as distinct from what we *think*

[1] *Philosophical Analysis.* (O.U.P., 1956.)

is our purpose) in using them? From this standpoint metaphysical statements could not be lightly dismissed; they had to be recognized as in some sense legitimate. But the philosophers who would have liked to dismiss them as meaningless were now constrained to argue that although they fulfil a variety of functions, and in this sense have meaning, they are not really statements of *fact*, even if we think they are. But by no means all philosophers have accepted this thesis. It is one thing to say that a certain metaphysical sentence cannot be taken as factual just as it stands, it is quite another to say that it has no factual content whatever. A view is emerging, and I think it correct, that *all* language has a metaphysical basis or, in other words, that all language expresses thoughts which pre-suppose some metaphysical picture or model or directive.

In two essays in a recently published symposium[1] the point is touched on. C. A. Mace, writing on "Some Trends in the Philosophy of Mind", shows that mental events are inevitably described in terms of "models". For example, Descartes used the model of the substance and its states. For Locke, the model was the container and its contents. And G. F. Stout once remarked that James Ward talked about the "I" as if it were an Eye. Mace comments that "all these models tend to be visual, and when we visualize them clearly they all look absurd. But not one of them is entirely absurd. Each draws attention to something of interest and importance. Absurdity results when some irrelevant features of the model are attributed to whatever is modelled." This seems to me a most penetrating observation, and the whole essay will repay study. S. Körner, in his essay in the same volume "Some Types of Philosophical Thinking", makes what I think is essentially

[1] *British Philosophy in the Mid-Century.* (George Allen & Unwin, 1957.)

the same point. All our thinking, he says, including our scientific thinking, is carried out in obedience to "metaphysical directives" which we give ourselves. They are "metaphysical" in the sense that they are too ultimate to be verified or falsified by events. He instances the basic divergence between Einstein and Born over the antithesis of law and chance. The point is that any sequence of events, however often repeated, can be ascribed to chance, while equally any sequence of events, however unusual, can be affirmed to be the expression of law. In neither case can the affirmation be falsified experimentally, and it is therefore metaphysical. Körner points out that a large part of Kant's work can be regarded as an attempt to make explicit hidden metaphysical directives to which *all* rational beings are committed.

The vital point here is that the use of *some* model, the following of *some* directive, i.e. the acceptance of *some* metaphysic, is inevitable. Even the logical positivist has to make some metaphysical assumptions before he can begin to talk about verification or falsification by events. If our aim in defining philosophy as the study of the way in which we operate with sentences is to exclude metaphysics we fail. For if this study includes decisions that some forms of factual sentence are preferable to others—preferable from the philosophical and not merely the literary standpoint—this must mean that they describe more adequately whatever it is that language is about. And since philosophy is not an experimental science, how can philosophers discuss whether one form of words is more adequate in this respect than another, except by discussing whether some model or directive is not in some respect *truer*—more adequate to the objective situation—than another? And if the analyst tries to evade this difficulty by denying that it is his job to decide that some sentences are preferable to others in their objective reference,

13

how is philosophical criticism to be distinguished from literary criticism? Is it worth bothering about, anyhow? The fact is, we cannot talk significantly about sentences at all unless we pre-suppose the existence of people who use the sentences to communicate their thoughts one to another and describe the world in which they live. But this is to pre-suppose a complex ontology, i.e. a doctrine of being, which cannot be verified or falsified by particular events—in short, a metaphysic. For if I choose as my model a solipsistic one—the view that I alone exist and that all my sensations are merely sensations and witness to no existence outside myself—no sensation can, in the nature of things, falsify my view.

Now the "model" with which the Christian is most fundamentally concerned is the God-model, and a question of great importance clearly arises. Are there no rational grounds on which one model or one directive is to be preferred to another? Is it merely a question of making an arbitrary choice where reason cannot help? The post-Kantian idealists had a clear answer to this; they had quite clear-cut criteria for choosing their model. The earlier analysts rejected their doctrine out of hand with their rejection of all constructive or metaphysical philosophy: the doctrine was not refuted, but dismissed. But there are indications that in the sixth decade of the century philosophers are being forced back to it. In a recently published symposium[1] Basil Mitchell, in his essay, "The Grace of God", speaks of our adopting "some device for co-ordinating our experiences—this being a deeply rooted instinct (the metaphysical instinct?)". Now "co-ordinating" here suggests that the criterion for accepting a model is the *order* it produces in what would otherwise be chaos—some measure of system, unity and coherence. This is one of the many indications of the reaction by later philosophers against

[1] *Faith and Logic.* (George Allen & Unwin, 1957.)

the assumption in Wittgenstein's *Tractatus* that the objective situation exhibits absolute plurality or atomism—entire absence of connection. J. R. Lucas, in his essay "The Soul" in the same volume, is even more explicit on the point. He writes "We are motivated by a general nisus towards the greatest simplification of our thought and discourse, and unification of our conceptual structure". But this basic directive towards unification is not our free creation, our explicit choice. It dominated our thinking long before we were aware of it. It is as much a brute fact as any of the sensuous facts to which the materialist appeals. It is far wiser to take it as a key to reality, or at any rate to follow it and see where it leads, than to dismiss it as subjective illusion. It is overwhelmingly probable that our "demand" for system rather than chaos, law rather than chance, is not merely an arbitrary demand but an insight. We shall find later that to obey this directive persistently, to follow the insight patiently, will lead us to Theism.

So far, in answering the charge that belief in God is not verifiable by sense-perception we have, in effect, replied "What of it? Belief is still reasonable." But a second answer is possible, and valid. We can insist that assertion of God's existence is *not*, in principle, unverifiable or unfalsifiable in human experience. In a recent book by Dr. E. L. Mascall[1] he shows that the contentions of certain contemporary philosophers show, progressively, an approach to the second answer. John Wisdom of Cambridge and R. M. Hare of Oxford have appeared more or less willing to argue on the basis that Christians will not allow *any* fact to falsify their belief, but in defence of Theism they pointed out that it nevertheless makes a vast difference to a man—and, presumably to his reaction to life—whether he believes in God or not. Wisdom

[1] *Words and Images.* (Longmans, Green & Co., 1957.)

said that the difference as to whether a God exists involves our *feelings*, and "in this respect is more like a difference as to whether there is beauty in a thing". Hare pointed out that theistic belief is much more than detached intellectual accept-ance. But B. G. Mitchell went further. He would not accept the charge that Christians allow no fact to *count* against the asser-tion that God loves men. Clearly there are facts which do count. But they do not count enough. The Christian's faith, based on the Christian experience, is strong enough to bear the strain. If asked what happenings would convince him that his faith was delusion, he refuses to answer. He will not put God to the test.

But *is* this the Christian's final answer? Would Christian experience be sufficient to sustain such a faith for ever if the facts continued to challenge it for ever—if there were never to be a verification? Here Dr. Mascall quotes I. M. Crombie: "Could anything count decisively against the view that God is merciful? Yes, suffering which was utterly, eternally and irredeemably pointless." But if human personality is extin-guished with the death of the body, suffering *is* pointless. Our belief in the existence of a good God is bound up with our belief that human personality can survive death. Jesus was quite sure of this. "God is not the God of the dead but of the living." And the Pauline-Johannine proof of the love of God is His gift of eternal life. Of course we cannot in the nature of things demonstrate by experiment here and now that we shall survive death, but this is not a *logical* or *linguistic* inability to verify survival; it is merely a *practical* difficulty. Those who verify to themselves their survival of physical death cannot (unless the spiritualists are right) communicate with us. But even in their first fine careless rapture the positivists admitted that for an assertion to be meaningful it need only *in principle* be capable of verification. It was not held that verification must be a practical possibility.

16

A comparison of the arguments of Wisdom, Hare, Mitchell and Crombie bring out, Dr. Mascall shows, a point of enormous importance. A. G. N. Flew pointed out that if we rely on the Wisdom arguments alone, what started as an assertion of fact—that God exists—is reduced to the status of a "picture preference", and that if we rely on the Hare argument alone, "no cosmological assertions about the nature and activities of a supposed personal creator" are involved. Mitchell and Crombie, however, insist that theological utterances about God *are* cosmological assertions; God exists *objectively*, independently of *our* existence. But this insistence is all the more necessary because a well-known philosopher has gone to the length of claiming that to be a Christian does not involve the acceptance of this objective interpretation of Christian utterances. R. B. Braithwaite[1] interprets statements about God as elliptical statements about men's experiences and attitudes. His view may be illustrated by two quotations: "I myself take the typical meaning of the body of Christian assertions as being given by their proclaiming intentions to follow an agapeistic way of life." He agrees that a religious assertion has a propositional element that is lacking in a moral assertion, in that it will refer to a story as well as manifest an intention. But this is only the telling of, or alluding to, the story "in the way in which one can tell, or allude to, the story of a novel with which one is acquainted".

The central argument of this book is in effect a refutation of Braithwaite's thesis. I shall start from the obvious point that I must either refuse to transcend my immediate here-and-now experience—refuse, that is, to make any ontological or existential assertions whatsoever on the basis of it—or else affirm that some entities exist. I shall make one important

[1] *An Empiricist's View of the Nature of Religious Belief.* (C.U.P., 1957.)

concession to the positivist, namely that my willingness to believe in my own existence as an entity transcending the present moment, and in the existence of other people, does not commit me to a *riot* of "reification"—does not commit me, that is, to the view that *every* noun that appears in human speech stands for a separately existing entity. The positivists, I hold, have a strong case if they confine their refusal to reify nouns to impersonal nouns. I shall argue for Berkeleian caution in the matter of reifying material-object-nouns, and shall show that relativistic and atomic physics provide an additional argument for such caution. But I shall insist that positivists have failed to see the vast implications of the fact that the one type of noun which we *must* reify is the person-noun. Every individual *knows* that other individuals who are thinking, sensing and feeling emotion exist "outside" him. Sentences like 'William is in pain' must be taken at their face value, however justified we may be in refusing to take at their face value sentences about alleged impersonal entities such as chairs or virtues and interpreting them as elliptical statements about our experiences. And I shall argue that the word 'God', although carrying, admittedly, a vastly different connotation from nouns standing for human beings, is very much more akin to such nouns than to scientific or material-object nouns. Even, then, if one accepts the positivistic analysis of impersonal sentences, one can consistently reify 'God', i.e. hold that a transcendent God exists.

But can one *prove* that God exists? Christian apologists have of late tended to defer quite unnecessarily to the philosophical analysts and the biblical theologians who, differing so vastly in all else, have joined in attacking metaphysical thinking. Christian rationalists have been far too hesitant and defensive in the matter. I have sometimes shuddered at the effect which must surely be produced in the minds of intelligent hearers when a preacher declares that God has revealed himself in the Bible or in human experience and then proceeds to *contrast* such revelation, as a proof of God, with human reasoning, adding that the human mind cannot discover valid reasons for believing in God. If there are no valid reasons for believing in God, there are equally no valid reasons for interpreting any human writings or experiences as His revelation. This applies both to the Barthian interpretation of experiences as confrontations by a God "outside" us and to the mystics' interpretation of their experiences as illuminations from a God "within" us. Apart from some measure of interpretation, a human experience is merely a *subjective* human experience; it signifies nothing. But interpretation involves rational construction, i.e. an integration of the experience into our general view of reality.

The trouble with the majority of Christian apologists is that, not being professional philosophers, they are not acutely aware of the necessity of distinguishing, when they talk of "proving" God's existence, between on the one hand the kind of reasoning which at one time was called "deductive" but which has latterly been described as "logically necessary" or "tautological", and, on the other hand, that constructive thinking which includes the inductions or empirical generalizations of science and of everyday life and also metaphysical construction. A further source of confusion is that so many of the professional philosophers who *are* well aware of this distinction find it convenient to ignore it when they are trying to refute arguments for Theism. Now let us agree that it is impossible to prove the existence of God by the first type of reasoning—by using logically necessary sentences alone. Does it follow that we are therefore unable to offer *any* proof of the existence of God? Certainly not, unless we decide, quite arbitrarily, to restrict the use of the word 'proof' to *logically* necessary proof. But if we do this last, it follows that we cannot prove *anything at all* about the real world! *All* our knowledge of the real world is based on observation (including experiment) and rational construction. None of it is logically necessary. I cannot "prove" God. Very well, but in that case I cannot "prove" anything at all about the real world; I cannot prove anything I care about—anything that matters. I cannot even prove that other people besides myself exist. For the denial that other people exist, however fantastically absurd, does not land me in self-contradiction. I can quite consistently refuse to regard my private sensations as witnessing to the existence of other people. And if I take that line, no sensation can falsify my belief.

But we can quite reasonably refuse to restrict the meaning of the word 'proof' to logically necessary proof. We can point out that scientists in their laboratories, barristers in the law-courts, politicians in Parliament and ordinary people in their homes and in the market-place are claiming every day that this or that statement can be taken as proved. And "to prove" a statement in this sense is to show that it "fits" or "accounts for" what we immediately experience, and that either no alternative theory can *in fact* be thought of or else that no *conceivable* alternative theory fits the facts so well. It is sheer bias, or muddle-headedness, to deny, in principle, that God's existence can in this valid sense of "prove" be proved. One has the right, of course, to criticize any *particular* proof of God's existence which is offered; one has the right to try to show that there are alternative intellectual constructions which account for the experienced data as well or better. But it is merely silly to try to rule out all proofs of God on the ground that no such proofs can be logically necessary ones. It will be one of my objects in what follows to show that the constructive proof of God's existence is as strong as many other beliefs which no one in practice dreams of doubting. A word must be added here to remove a misunderstanding. It is sometimes said that whereas a logically necessary proof is certain, constructive reasoning (including scientific induction) gives us at best a high degree of probability. This is not so. Constructive reasoning (implicit or explicit) can yield conclusions about which intelligent people do not and need not feel the slightest uncertainty. A man is, and is right in being, as certain that other people exist, including his wife, and that she loves him, as he is of the validity of the proof of Pythagoras's theorem. And a person who is both intellectually *and* emotionally mature—a person who enjoys something of that wide range of experience which inspires the testimony of prophets, poets and mystics and who is capable of constructive thought, can feel *absolutely* sure of God.

We now come to the second of the three analytical attacks —the denial by recent philosophers, following C. L. Stevenson, that sentences about right and wrong and sentences using 'ought' and 'duty', are statements about objective fact, and their consequent proposal to treat these statements as veiled exhortations, or as merely expressions of emotions and attitudes. In an extremely interesting essay in the symposium *British Contemporary Philosophy in the Mid-Century*[1] by Dr. A. C. Ewing on recent developments in British ethical thought, he contends that "such modes of analysis fail to give anything like an adequate account of what we mean, in the ordinary straightforward sense of 'mean', when we make what we call 'ethical judgments' in our daily practical life". Dr. Ewing is clearly right; we certainly mean that our statements are objectively true; we mean that certain actions are right and others wrong, and that if every finite being in existence thought otherwise this would not alter the facts. The state-

[1] George Allen & Unwin, 1957.

ment 'cruelty is wrong' is in this respect far more like 'three twos make six' or 'arsenic is poisonous' than it is like 'blondes are preferable to brunettes'. The Stevensonians have no right to tell us what we mean; *we* are the best judges of that. Their only course, Dr. Ewing points out, is to say that the common-sense view of ethical judgments is muddled, and that they are giving the nearest view of it which can be intelligibly and consistently stated. It seems to me that this goes to the heart of the matter. The subjectivist moralist can state a case if he is prepared to say frankly that the meaning we all attach to our ethical judgments is a *wrong* meaning. This will involve him in a metaphysical argument about the relation of our thinking to reality. But he cannot win a short and easy victory for subjectivism by pretending to analyse ethical sentences.

In actual fact, the Stevensonians' account of ethical judg-ments is based on what Dr. Ewing calls their "general epis-temological assumptions" or—what comes to the same thing —on their implicit acceptance of a certain type of metaphysi-cal model or directive. Subjectivist moral philosophers are sure that moral judgments *cannot* be objective because they assume objective reality to be of such a nature as could not "house" objective moral valuations. If the "ultimate" realities —whatever that means—are particles or bundles of energy or logical atoms or sensa, then moral values *cannot* be objective. But most people who feel strongly on moral issues will prob-ably think it far more likely that moral values are objective than that ultimate reality consists of particles, etc. In short, instead of rejecting objective morality because it does not square with some particular metaphysical theory, we have a right to reject any metaphysical theory which cannot house objective morality. If the only way of housing it is in Objective Mind or Will—i.e. in God, so be it.

There has of late been in certain quarters an attempt to

by-pass the matter of moral objectivity by suggesting that the only significant, or the only important, or the only soluble problems about right and wrong are the psychological ones. Those who hold this view have pointed out that a person's moral opinions and reactions are determined not by any explicit decision that moral judgments are objective or by the acceptance of any criterion for deciding what is right and what wrong, but by the training and influences to which he is subjected during childhood and adolescence. We need not dispute this last as a statement about human psychology, and it does not need the notion of conditioned reflexes to commend it. Talk about conditioned reflexes, indeed, is only an attempt to draw a physiological picture corresponding to psychological facts which were known long before these reflexes were heard of. But this attempt to side-track the philosophical issues is futile. The mere statement of the fact that person A *can* influence the morality of person B does not answer A's question: "In what direction *shall* I influence B's morality?" or even "How *ought* I to do so?" This question is a philosophical one, and in a thorough investigation of it the matter of the objectivity of moral judgments cannot be ignored. Moreover, human beings are self-conscious; there comes a time when B becomes explicitly aware that his whole system of moral sentiments is what it is because he has been trained and influenced since childhood, or because, if you prefer, his reflexes have been conditioned, and that if he had been otherwise influenced his moral outlook would be different. But to become aware of this is to become "free" to continue or reverse the moral trends of his life. He can consciously decide to behave as those who influenced him meant him to behave, or he can revolt. And surely, if he comes to regard his moral convictions as *merely* the results of society's efforts to make him subordinate his interests to *its* interests, he will feel no strong emotional urge to comply. Why indeed should he, since for him words like 'ought', 'right' and 'wrong' have been emptied of all objective reference?

The real problem, then, is to find a moral motive which can be explicitly stated to a person who has come to self-consciousness and can no longer be subconsciously or unconsciously conditioned. This is a philosophical problem—or a religious one.

The third of the attacks on the Christian faith to which I referred at the beginning of this section is the attempt to reduce language about mental processes to language about bodily processes or dispositions. This is a twentieth-century version of nineteenth-century "scientific materialism". With the pure Watsonian behaviourism of the early years of the century, the difficulty of most people was to understand how anyone could believe anything so silly. One's modesty at first compelled one to assume that the behaviourists really meant something subtle which eluded one, and it was with some reluctance that one was forced at last to admit that there existed apparently intelligent people who really thought that statements about people's seeing or hearing were merely statements in other words about how the particles of their bodies were moving! C. A. Mace, in his essay referred to earlier, refers to this early crude form of behaviourism as "a rather vulgar iconoclastic revolution". "There are, it was baldly stated, no minds, no thoughts, no mental images, no dreams or nightmares, no feelings, no desires. There is nothing, nothing, nothing, but bodies and their responses to stimulation."

One would have thought that once this nonsense was seen through, philosophers would have dropped the whole thing and accepted consciousness as fundamental—as the basic fact in terms of which one's philosophizing must be conducted.

But this would have run counter to prejudices which have operated very powerfully in this century. What actually ensued in certain quarters was an attempt to save as much as possible from the wreck. Dr. Mace refers to the next stage as "dispositional behaviourism". The claim that when a man perceives, remembers, imagines, or desires, all that is taking place is that his body and his body-particles are in motion, was dropped. There was substituted the claim that "To perceive something . . . is to be *disposed* to behave in a certain way". And when philosophy became explicitly analytical, the obvious thing was to claim that a correct analysis of statements about mental happenings was a statement about bodily dispositions.

But this attempt to banish the notion of mental events has been rather half-hearted. Reservations had obviously to be made, and if there can be mental events *at all, cadit quaestio*. We clearly do not have to wait to see how we act before we can know what we are thinking and feeling. And it does make sense to say that I saw the force of an argument at one o'clock. But even if, *per impossibile*, it could be shown that what one is immediately aware of when one introspects is bodily happenings, one has still not banished consciousness. For one has had to use the words "one is . . . aware"!

Nevertheless, the dissatisfaction of philosophers with common-sense language about "bodies" and "minds" is well grounded. There is something fundamentally wrong with the notion that a man consists of two co-ordinate entities which act and react on one another—a bodily machine and a psychical ghost. I shall justify this statement in what follows, and here I will merely record my conviction that one of the greatest tasks before Christian philosophers is a correct analysis of body-mind language. I have tried in this book to make some contribution to this task.

25

2

LINGUISTIC ANALYSIS AND IDEALISM

There is a notion abroad in the Western world that the writings of the physical scientist are descriptions of reality, whereas those of the poet, the prophet and the religious thinker are descriptions of subjective emotions, impressions or visions, and that whereas religion deals in edifying myths, science achieves objective truth. I propose to subject this notion to a sustained criticism in what follows, in the course of which I shall show that the language used by the physicist, the astronomer and the cosmogonist has no claim whatever to "correspond" to, or to describe, reality in the simple way which common sense imagines, whereas language which uses the word 'God', although admittedly anthropomorphic, has in one vital respect a claim to objectivity which the language of the physical sciences has not.

I have been prompted to write this book by the conviction that theists have, in the present century, been far too hesitant, and far too much on the defensive. Most of those who profess disbelief in God have a more or less definite belief as to the nature of reality, and this is open to devastating attack. Most non-Christian scientists and "plain men" in western countries have a naïve faith in the existence of a spatio-temporal framework in which the basic realities are bits of matter or of energy, and they endow these with the capacity to "produce" conscious life by blind chance or by the operation of impersonal "laws". Consistently with this belief, the "basic reality"—whatever that means—of a man is regarded as constituted by his physical organism, and his consciousness is regarded as a by-product which could not possibly survive the body's death. Christian apologists have always, of course, criticized this picture of reality, but far too gently. They have tended to concede far too much to it. Their basic mistake has been to endeavour to *supplement* it by saying that although it contains a large measure of truth there are "spiritual values" existing alongside of all this material reality. This is a tactical error. We should never concede the self-existence of the spatio-temporal framework and its alleged contents. If we do, the most we can hope for is that "spiritual values" will be tolerated as more or less irrelevant—as alien to the essence of things. We should go over to the offensive, and attack the whole theory, root and branch. To accept it naïvely is to display a credulity compared with which a belief in fairies is hard-bitten realism.

I am not, of course, seeking to disparage science *as such*. It would be absurd to try to "de-bunk" a human activity which has provided us with instruments so potent for good or ill. My aim is merely to give the concepts of the physical sciences their correct "logical geography"—to use Professor Ryle's phrase.[1] It is true that my main argument on this point contains an implied criticism of certain statements by scientists who have wandered into philosophy or theology, but this is no criticism of scientists as such.

I shall select two main types of sentence and shall show that while we can reasonably claim that true statements of the one

[1] *The Concept of Mind*, page 8,

type describe the objective situation with directness and simplicity, no such claim can be made for true statements of the other type. It will follow that while each type can legitimately be used in separation from the other, the mixture of the two types, in the way that everyday language does mix them, results in confusion and gives rise to pseudo-problems. It will follow that when we are philosophizing we should always be acutely aware of this, and that *constructive* philosophy must use the first type of language, and avoid the misleading suggestions of the second type or of a mixture of the two. I shall then show that language about God is legitimately derived from the first type of language, and shall indicate the bearing of my thesis on the questions of human free-will and the survival of human personality after death. Finally I shall discuss the relation between my conclusions and certain central Christian affirmations.

The generous use of inverted commas in a book which deals with the relation of language to reality is regrettable but inevitable. One must make it clear whether one is talking of the words themselves or of the things for which they are supposed to stand. The commas will be used singly to indicate that I am referring to words or sentences as symbols. For example, I shall discuss whether 'chair' stands for a real chair. The use of double commas will mean either that I am quoting or that I am using language which is probably open to criticism but which I do not want to stop to criticize. In the latter case the inverted commas will more or less serve the purpose of a parenthetical "so to speak" or "as we say". But I do not claim to have been quite consistent in the choice of single or double commas, for there are border-line cases.

To any reader acquainted with the history of philosophy it will soon become apparent that my division of language into these two main types has an intimate relation to what is perhaps the most important controversy that has engaged the attention of philosophers during the last two hundred years— the idealist-realist controversy. I do not share the view sometimes expressed of late that everything has been said on the subject that *can* be said, nor the view that the controversy has been shown by linguistic analysis to be "merely verbal". I wish, however, to make it clear at the outset that although I may be said to favour idealism in the sense of calling attention to what I regard as the essence of the idealist case and pointing out how valuable and irrefutable this is, there are, nevertheless, a number of propositions commonly attributed, fairly or not, to idealists as a class which I should certainly not wish to defend. For example, I would not affirm "the identity of knower and object known", nor would I say that thinking, as such, creates or even alters its own objects.

My reasons for rejecting the suggestion that analysis has shown the idealist-realist controversy to be merely verbal will appear in the course of the argument, but something may be said at once. Even if no particular events in the so-called material world around us can be seen to be relevant to the truth or the falsity of the idealist's contention, it does not follow that the controversy is merely linguistic. For the controversy is certainly relevant to one's emotional and practical reaction to life. For example, if anyone is impressed by the alleged "vastness" of the Universe and the relative "littleness" of man, and disposed on that score to draw depressing conclusions as to his nature and destiny, or if anyone is disposed to believe that "matter" is a sort of primary reality and that our mental processes are therefore related to our bodily processes much in the way that a flame is related to a candle and that therefore we cannot survive the death of our bodies, the essential insight of idealism, once he shares it, will show him how groundless is his pessimism.

One of the most characteristic features of the idealist-realist controversy is that the opponents so rarely get to real grips. The most prominent attempts to refute idealism in recent years have concerned themselves with propositions which do not seem to me to express the really basic idealist contention. These realist attacks seem to be based on the assumption that the idealist case is so inherently untenable that it is quite unnecessary to try to get, so to speak, inside the idealist's skin. Now an unwillingness to try, patiently and sympathetically, to get to the heart of the belief of a large number of admittedly distinguished thinkers is itself a phenomenon calling for investigation, and I suggest that in dismissing idealism so summarily people are misled by a certain mental picture.

Let us suppose that a person looks out of his window and sees a man looking at a house. Let us suppose that he sees the man turn round and walk away, and can therefore be sure that the man no longer sees the house. The person looking from the window, however, still sees the house, and may therefore say "I cannot dispute the evidence of my senses. The house is quite unaffected by the fact that the man is no longer perceiving it." Now it is this appeal to "the evidence of our senses" which makes people feel, when they first read some account of what idealists are supposed to believe, that there *must* be something wrong in the idealist's case, and which therefore prevents them from approaching the subject with an open mind. I shall now show that the evidence of the senses, thus appealed to, does not thus decide the issue out of hand. It *sets* the problem, it does not *solve* it.

What precisely is it that our example of the man seeing a second man looking at a house can rationally lead us to infer? To begin with, let us examine the sentence "two people are looking at the same object". This does not mean that what they sense or perceive is exactly the same or exactly similar. One may see a circle and another an ellipse. Now we certainly cannot dispose of the subject by saying that although they perceive different percepts the percepts are nevertheless "percepts of the same object", or by saying that the one "sees it as" a circle, the other as an ellipse. This is merely to set the problem, not to solve it. For the idealist-realist controversy is concerned with this very question—what is the meaning of the phrase 'percepts of the same object' and the phrase 'sees it as . . .'? The realist does not go to the length of claiming that a circle is the same as an ellipse; he admits the difference *in the percepts*. And the idealist, for his part, does not deny that the one person's circular percept is related in a very special way to the other person's elliptical percept. The question at issue is this: what is the best way of accounting for certain facts about what we perceive—for example, the fact that our percepts occur in an order which we can control only in a limited degree, and that one person's percepts are correlated with those of other persons?

Now this being so, it is clear that no short and easy appeal to "the evidence of our senses" can decide the issue. The evidence of our senses in the matter of the two persons and the house is merely evidence that if one person's percepts correspond to those of another person in the way that we describe as "being percepts of the same material object", then the disappearance of one person's percepts from his field of vision need not affect the corresponding percepts in the other person's field of vision. But that fact is as patent to the idealist as to the realist, and clearly does *not* in itself settle the controversy over the meaning of the phrase "percepts of the same material object". What is at issue, as we shall see, is whether it is significant, and if significant true, to say that "material objects exist in themselves" or "by themselves", i.e. not as objects-of-consciousness. The fact that a percept can vanish from Jones's field of perception without the corresponding percept vanishing from Smith's field of perception is very far from proving that it is true, or even significant, to say that our percepts are caused by or related to a "material object" which exists "in itself" or "on its own".

I have written enough to show that the picture of two persons looking at "the same object", which at first sight appears to settle our controversy in favour of the realist, does not really do so. It is probable, however, that even many professional philosophers have not entirely escaped its influence—an influence all the greater for not being realized. It is hard, otherwise, to account for the cavalier—not to say slipshod—way in which idealism is often treated, when it is not ignored. We shall never get to the root of the issue between idealist and realist unless we see clearly that while realism has derived its appearance of self-evidence from the sort of example we have considered, idealism is derived from quite another type of example. The realist starts from *another* person's seeing an object; the idealist starts from *his own* seeing of it. The extreme importance of this difference of starting-point will become clear as we proceed.

Let us begin by assuming that we know what we mean when we say that a word "stands for" or "refers to" or "represents" an object—when we say, for example, that the word-symbol 'Mr. Brown' represents the real Mr. Brown. Let us, further, define as a 'complete symbol' a word or phrase which stands for an entity which exists "by itself", or "on its own" or "independently", and not as an abstract feature of a more concrete whole. And let us define as a 'partial symbol' a word or phrase which is not, in the above sense, a complete symbol. A partial symbol is, thus, one which does not stand for a concrete or separately existing entity.[1]

Let us begin by considering the phrase 'The shape and the matter of this vase'. It is clear that the symbols 'shape' and 'matter' in this phrase are not complete symbols in the above sense. We know of no entity which is just a shape; there is always something which *has* the shape. And we cannot conceive of any actual piece of matter as having no shape whatever. If, therefore, we allow ourselves to speak of the word 'shape' or the word 'matter', in a sentence which distinguishes shape from matter, as "standing for" anything—in the sense of any *thing*—we say that this "thing" is an "abstraction". But we do not take this language seriously; we do not believe that an abstraction *is* a thing that can exist "on its own". To do so would be to commit the error of "reifying" or "hypostatizing" an abstraction. We do not really think that when the rest of Alice's cat vanished, the grin could remain "on its own". It is, however, of the utmost importance to see that in denying that a shape or that shapeless matter or that a grin can exist "on its own", *we are not denying its reality*. The vase has a *real* shape; its shape is *really* embodied in its matter; a cat *really does* have a certain kind of look on its face.

Now I am going to show that just as the word 'matter' (in a sentence contrasting matter with shape) and the word 'shape' stand for abstractions, i.e. they are partial symbols and abstract nouns, so in the sentence 'I am perceiving a vase-percept' the words 'I' and 'vase-percept' stand for abstractions (which does *not*, as we have just seen, mean that they do not stand for realities or that "the ego is an illusion" or that "the vase does not exist"). From this it will follow that just as

---

[1] I choose the term 'partial' rather than 'incomplete' so as to avoid confusion with a rather different use of the word 'incomplete' as applied to symbols. (See, for example, J. O. Urmson's *Philosophical Analysis* (Oxford, 1956), page 56.)

there cannot be shape without matter and matter without shape so there cannot be a perceiving ego without percepts or percepts without a perceiving ego. To show this will not, of course, prove that a *vase-in-itself* cannot exist "out there", quite independently of any consciousness of it; I have not yet come to *that* question. I am at this stage concerned merely with analysing what is "in" human experience, not with what is "outside" it. I am deliberately holding open for the moment the question of the existence of the vase-in-itself. I am starting from the point on which we are all agreed, namely that we perceive an object-of-perception, and in calling what we perceive a 'percept' I am not prejudging the question whether the percept represents something which can exist out of relation to an ego. I am merely asking the reader to exercise a little patience, and examine carefully the experience itself before discussing whether anything, and if so what, can be said about something "outside" it.

Let us first consider whether the symbol 'I' in the sentence 'I am perceiving a vase-percept' is a complete or a partial symbol, and then consider the bearing of our conclusion on the question whether 'vase-percept' is a complete or partial symbol. The percept, or what is being perceived, is certainly perceived as extended, but who would affirm that the perceiving was a little to the left of the percept, or was in front of it, and that it was a small perceiving? And where do we locate what 'I' stands for? It would be absurd to try to locate it anywhere, even in the percept which I call my "body", for this body-percept is part of my perceptual continuum; from the point of view of our analysis of perception the body-percept is just one percept among others, such as the table or the moon. To locate whatever is indicated by 'I' in the body-percept would, therefore, be as nonsensical as to locate it in table-percept or in the moon-percept.

34

An objection may here be made. "What you are saying of the body", it may be urged, "is true so far as visual perceptions of your body are concerned. You are justified in maintaining that the only point of difference between your *seen* body and the seen table or moon is that your *seen* body always occupies, more or less, the centre of your visual field. You are justified in holding that this does not prevent its being an object, just as much as are the table and the moon. But you are also aware of your body by organic, including kinaesthetic, sensations, and psychologists regard these as the basis, or at any rate part of the basis, of one's self-awareness." My answer is this. I do not deny that it is possible to be aware of one's body by that process which G. F. Stout called "internal perception". Nor would I deny that, for example, the organic and kinaesthetic sensations accompanying the movement of one's eyes in focusing them on to an object, tend to be regarded as constituents of that loosely-defined entity which may be called the bodily or the empirical self. But this is quite irrelevant to the point I am making. So far as its relation to whatever is indicated by 'I' is concerned, the bodily self or the empirical self is as much an object as is the moon. The *psychological* distinction between self and notself breaks out within the *object* of cognition. It is quite different from the distinction between cognitive subject and cognitive object. The sentences 'I see the table', 'I feel the warmth of the sun', 'I feel organic and kinaesthetic sensations', have precisely the same logical form, and the word 'I' functions in the same way in all three. This abundantly justifies my statement that it is as absurd to locate whatever is indicated by 'I' in my body as in the moon. What 'I' indicates is not to be identified with any percept, any sensation, whatsoever, even the most subtle "inner" or bodily feeling, nor with any number or combination of them. It indicates, however, an essential characteristic

35

of the whole experience—a characteristic which is as *real* as any object.

To see this last is to see the absurdity of the assertion "there is no self", with which the followers of Hume have concluded this sort of analysis.[1] Not being able to point to any particular sensation or feeling or to anything localized anywhere and to say "That is myself" they proceeded to say, in effect, "there is no self and therefore it can have no cognitive function; there is only a succession or aggregation of separate sensations, feelings and images", and just because they could not isolate by introspection a feeling of perceiving, some of them denied that there was any real perceiving-function. But all this was to assume that the use of symbols such as 'I' and 'perceive' can be justified only if each can be shown to stand, all by itself, for some particular entity or event. This is nonsense. We have already noticed that the word 'shape' does not stand for a separate entity but only for an abstraction; and yet bodies really *are* shaped. To justify the use of the words 'I' and 'perceive' you have only to show that they perform an indispensable function in sentences. You justify their use by challenging anyone to say in English exactly the same thing as "I perceive a vase" without using the partial symbols 'I' and 'perceive' or some other partial symbols which perform the same function.

Now all attempts by philosophers to show that for a sentence commencing with "I perceive . . ." or "I know that . . ." one can substitute a sentence which means the same but which omits a verb of cognition and the 'I' have broken down. The Humians have failed to see the very great difference between

---

[1] An example of this mistake occurs in Wittgenstein's *Tractatus* (5.631) "The thinking, presenting subject. There is no such thing." But post-Kantian idealists who insisted on the reality of the subject of awareness did not claim that it was a *thing* existing apart from what it cognized

on the one hand saying that *there occur* sense-data or images which are *in fact* similar in shape and different in colour, and on the other hand saying "*I know* (or *he knows*) *that* this is similar to that in shape and different in colour". Again, to say "I notice that A is followed by B" is not merely to say "A occurs and then B occurs" or even "I notice A and then I notice B". What has occurred is that the succession of A by B has *itself* been noticed, and we cannot accurately record a noticing of any complex without using a form of language which records the unity of the total knowledge-process. This is the function of 'I'. To say "I know that . . ." or "I notice that . . ." is to say it in the simplest, most ultimate and irreducible terms. We can *conceive* of the ego and its functions but we must guard against the temptation to try to *visualize* them. We must not, for example, try to "see" the successive experiences of one ego as a succession of visible entities in a row, and then try to image the ego and its functions by a line connecting them. All such pictures are misleading. It is absurd to try to represent by an object what is not an object, to visualize by a particular what is not a particular. And when, as in the case before us, the question at issue is whether a word can function properly if it does not stand for a particular percept or feeling, one is clearly begging the question when one answers "No" merely because one cannot visualize a particular percept or feeling for which it stands!

Since writing the above I have read, in Chapter V of Professor C. A. Campbell's Gifford Lectures[1] his admirable discussion of self-consciousness and self-identity. With his main thesis I am in complete agreement; the self is not *reducible* to its experiences. But I do not think it necessary to describe the self as (page 82) "a being which is distinct from the states in which it manifests itself". I think the thesis for which he is

---

[1] *On Selfhood and Godhood.* (George Allen & Unwin, 1957.)

contending is more securely based if we confine ourselves to saying that the sentence in which a personal pronoun is followed by a verb of cognition or of activity ("I see . . .", "I know that . . .", "He chooses to . . .", "I did so-and-so") is in its most ultimate and irreducible form. References to the self as "a being" which is "distinct" but which "manifests" itself may lead our readers or hearers, if it has not led us, to try to visualize the situation. It seems to me that there is a hankering after visualization when one sees a *problem* in the fact that the subject indicated by 'I' retains identity amid a plurality and a succession of experiences. The task before the philosopher—at least, *one* of his tasks—is to find the most appropriate, ultimate and irreducible language in which to *describe* whatever we are concerned with at the moment. The feeling that the so-called "relation of the self to its experiences" needs "explaining" is, I suggest, a desire to have a mental picture, an analogy from the world of *objects*, of a situation which transcends mere objects. In the nature of things this is impossible. I cannot follow Professor Campbell, then, when he says that although it is meaningful to talk about the self and its experiences this is not the same thing as claiming that it is intelligible, in the sense of capable of being understood. He thinks that we could claim that the self was intelligible only if we could "understand *how* it remains one amid the plurality of its changing experiences". This looks to me like demanding a picture. I suggest that when we use language about one and the same person being aware of a plurality and succession of objects, remembering "past" experiences and remaining the same throughout a period of time, we have reached the obvious limit of language and that the demand for an explanation—a demand "how" this can be—is not a demand that we can significantly make. We have reached the limit of human language and there is nothing more to be said.

Indeed, if we are asked whether *anything* can be said to be identical although it changes, and how it achieves this, the reasonable answer is "The *self* is identical amid change, and the only way to see *how* it does it is to be self-conscious". In fairness to Professor Campbell, however, I must add that he was probably aiming, in different language, at the same point. For on page 108 he says: "I may here confess to a good deal of doubt whether in the end it really makes sense for finite beings to ask how they are what they are."

It is clear from the preceding discussion that in the sentence 'I am perceiving a vase-percept' the word 'I' does not stand for a particular entity which exists side-by-side with the vase-percept and could exist without it. The word 'I' performs an indispensable function in sentences as indicating the unity of perception; it shows that the percepts for which the object-nouns stand belong to one and the same duration-and-extension continuum. To see this clearly is to see something of vital importance to my whole argument, namely that a cognition-event[1] is a close and complex unity. An awareness of temporal succession is far more than a temporal succession of awareness; an awareness of spatial juxtaposition is far more than a spatial juxtaposition of awarenesses. The unity of the experience, indicated by 'I', and the plurality of the experience, indicated by the grammatical object or object-phrase, are mutually involved, and the involvement is logical. In the sentence 'I perceive an extended and changing perceptual field' the symbol 'I' and the symbol 'an extended and changing perceptual field' are related to each other, in one respect, in the same way as are the symbols 'shape' and 'matter' in the phrase 'The shape and matter of the vase'. In neither case

---

[1] I use this clumsy phrase in order to avoid the phrase "*act* of cognition". I ought not to use the term "act" without entering on a discussion which would complicate the point at issue unnecessarily.

does the pair of symbols stand for a pair of separate entities; in both cases they stand for a pair of logically involved abstractions. 'I' stands for the unity of the perceptual experience, while 'an extended and changing perceptual field' stands for its plurality. We refer to the unity-aspect as the "subjective" aspect and to the plurality-aspect as the "objective" aspect. To describe the concrete process of perceiving a vase we need the whole sentence 'I perceive a vase-percept'; we need, that is, to refer both to subject and experienced object. For the words 'I' and 'vase-percept' are partial symbols; they do not stand for concrete, separate entities or events. They stand for abstract features of a highly complex unity. A person is not a bare ego, without content, detached from what he cognizes. He is a concrete being, and the stuff of his being is a continuum of percepts, thoughts, imaginings, emotions and volitions. Language about the "subject" of his experience is language about the unifying principle of this whole—that which justifies us in speaking of "a person". The unifying principle or subject cannot rationally be conceived to exist without that of which it is the unifying principle, and equally the emotions and volitions, and also the percepts, must always be those of some ego.[1]

We have now reached a very important conclusion, namely that *percepts are as organically integrated in the unity of one's personal life as are one's emotions and volitions*. It is impossible to exaggerate the importance of this. Let us consider the case of a person before whose mind there is a certain percept (let

[1] This conclusion does not provide an argument against the possibility of our surviving the death of our bodies. No one is concerned to argue for the survival of an abstract ego. Survival of death means the extension of the memory-chain beyond the point of physical death. Indeed, our conclusion *supports* belief in survival in so far as it insists on the unity of the person, as against the Humian attempt to dissolve him into a loose aggregate of disconnected event.

us say the percept of a ship) which arouses in him the emotion of disappointment and prompts him to an important decision involving courage. And let us suppose that, in recording the state of his mind at this moment, we use the sentence 'His courage was extraordinary', or the sentence 'His disappointment was profound'. Now the form of these sentences might tend to suggest that courage was a sort of entity capable of existing by itself and having the quality of being extraordinary, just as Jones is an entity having the quality of being courageous. Similarly the form of sentence suggests that disappointment was a self-existent entity having the quality of being profound. But if someone attributed any such belief to us, we should hasten to explain that we "do not take these sentences literally" or that we do not reify or hypostatize the nouns 'courage' and 'disappointment'. Disappointment does not exist as a kind of *substance* outside the unity of a conscious experience. And if it was pointed out to us that we compare examples of courage of various people in differing circumstances, and record the result in some such wide generalization as 'Courage is valuable', we should reply that this does not prove that courage is an entity. We use the noun 'courage' to indicate the abstract common feature of a variety of concrete experiences or events.

All this, of course, is very elementary. But I have laboured it in view of our conclusion that percepts are as logically integrated into the unity of our personal lives as are our emotions and volitions. For it will now be clear that all that we have said about sentences the grammatical subjects of which are words like 'courage' must apply to sentences the grammatical subjects of which are words like 'ship' or 'chair'. If, on the ground that there is no self-existent courage-entity, the sentence 'Courage is valuable' must be analysed as 'People who are courageous are valuable to their fellows', so, on the

41

ground that a ship-percept cannot exist apart from the unity of a conscious experience, the sentence 'This ship has three masts' must be analysed into a sentence about people who do or will or may enjoy a three-masted-ship-percept.

But here an objection will certainly be raised. The objector will remind me that my analysis was made on one very important condition, namely that I was concerned to analyse the experience itself—the experience *alone*, and that I explicitly stated that I was not, for the moment, concerned with the existence or non-existence of material objects *in themselves*, or "outside" our experience of them. This being so, all that I am now entitled to claim is that the statement 'This ship-percept is a three-masted ship-percept' must be given an analysis similar to that of the statement 'Courage is valuable'. But no realist, it will be said, need object to that. No one believes that ship-percepts and chair-percepts float about on their own, outside the unity of a conscious experience. In this respect the word 'ship-percept' is like the word 'courage'; neither of them must be reified. But what you are claiming, it will be said, is not merely that the statement 'This *ship-percept* is a three-masted ship-percept', but that the statement 'This *ship* has three masts', must be given an analysis similar to the analysis of sentences about courage and disappointment, and accordingly replaced by sentences about people perceiving the ship. This, it will be said, does not follow from the analysis of experience which you have made.

The objection, however, misfires because it misconceives the nature of the argument. It is important, however, for the objection to be mentioned, for we are now enabled to see clearly what the argument is. There might be some point in pressing the objection if I were claiming to present a logically necessary proof that no material objects *could* exist "in themselves". But that is not my claim. It is as impossible for the idealist to offer a logically necessary proof that material objects do not exist "in themselves" as it is for the realist to offer a similar proof that they do. My argument is merely this. Having, in the course of our analysis, seen that ship-percepts and chair-percepts are as logically integrated into the unity of conscious experience as are emotions and volitions, *we are doing the same sort of thing* when we tear the chair-percept out of its living context and declare that a chair which resembles a chair-percept exists "in itself" as when we tear disappointment out of its living context and declare that there is a disappointment-entity existing "in itself".

Let us consider this closely. Smith and Brown and Robin-son are, in ordinary language, "looking at the same penny". Smith sees it, we say, as a circle, Brown sees it as an oval, Robinson sees it on edge as a thin, straight strip. But actu-ally, Smith's immediate experience is the seeing of a circle, Brown's the seeing of an oval, and Robinson's the seeing of a strip. But if they are not idealists, they regard the circle, the oval and the strip as still existing as a circle, an oval and a strip "outside" or independent of their experiences. It is probably true that if they could be efficiently cross-examined by a hostile counsel their views as to exactly *what* exists in itself would be found confused and mutually inconsistent. Indeed, one of them, sorely pressed, might admit that he really didn't know *what* existed except that it was an X about which all that could be said was that it was the sufficient rea-son of their each seeing the shape they did see. But this would be to withdraw the realist claim and to concede all that the idealist requires for a starting-point of his construction. For he could then contend that 'X' equals 'God'. But if they per-sisted in their realist attitude, they would have to claim that "outside" all conscious experience there exist circles and ovals and strips similar to those existing "in" experience, and this is the view I am attacking. And I am attacking it in the sense of showing that those who believe it have just as much and just as little logical justification as they would have if they claimed that courage and disappointment were entities exist- ing "on their own". If I insist on taking literally the sentence 'Courage is valuable', then I must hold either that there is a courage-entity independent of all persons which is neither Smith's courage nor Brown's courage nor Robinson's cour- age but the *common feature* of all three, or else that there is a courage-entity which is the *sum total* of the particular cour- ages. If this contention, in either form, is absurd, so is the contention that there exists "in itself" an entity which is either the common feature of the various seen shapes or else the sum total of the lot. And the absurdity results from the same fact—that what is indicated by the percept-word is as logically connected with what is indicated by the personal pronoun 'I' or 'he' as is what is indicated by the emotion-word or the volition-word. This logical connection or involvement is the same as that which connects or involves what is indicated by the word 'shape' with what is indicated by the word 'matter'; there cannot be shapeless matter or matter-less shape.

That then is the argument. Its very modesty is its strength. It says, in effect: "By all means affirm that material objects exist in themselves. I should not dream of trying to show that you are contradicting yourself. But at any rate face the fact that what you are doing is as defensible or as indefensible as asserting that shapes exist *as shapes* in themselves out of their logical involvement in shaped objects, or in shaped coloured patches or in sensations of felt shape. And the strength of my refusal to reify material-object words lies in the fact that I can never be shown to be wrong. That is what realists find so annoying about idealists. In the nature of things they cannot be refuted by appeal to particular experiences or experiments, and provided they state their analysis in the cautious way I have shown, there are simply no holes in it. For they are simply replacing sentences the grammatical subjects of which are material-object-nouns by sentences the grammatical subjects of which are personal nouns or pronouns. And it is always perfectly *safe* to do this. It cannot, in the nature of things, be *wrong* to do so.

But I must now deal with a further objection. "You are ignoring", someone may say, "the essential difference between percepts and emotions—between cognition and affective states. An emotion is admittedly part of the very stuff of a person's existence, but an act of perception, although from the standpoint of psychology an event "in" a person's mind and in this sense part of the stuff of his being, must also be regarded, as it *is* regarded by the science of logic and by the theory of knowledge, as carrying an *essential* reference to an object *other than itself*. It *is* a particular psychological event in a mind, but it is more; it postulates an objective reality. I cannot, therefore, agree to your claim that percepts and emotions and volitions are, so to speak, on the same level."

The objection is a serious one, and I shall consider it carefully. It recalls to one's mind the charge brought against the treatment of cognition by Berkeley and Hume that it is psychology rather than philosophy. But this objection certainly cannot be brought against post-Kantian idealism. The idealists of this later succession were acutely aware of the objective reference of cognition, and went, indeed, to the length—quite justified in my view—of insisting that the unit of cognition is the *judgment*—a judgment of which the *real* subject, as distinct from the grammatical subject, is Reality. It is, then, common ground among us that although a cognitive event is a momentary happening in someone's mind it "refers" to an objective situation other than itself. But the question at issue is as to the *nature* of that objective whole to which all cognition, as recorded in factual sentences, refers. And I must insist that whatever more than an event in a mind a cognitive event is, the fact that it *is* an event in a mind must not be overlooked when we consider the nature of that objective reality which cognition as such postulates.

Now to say that all cognition, as such, refers to reality is by no means to close the discussion before us—still less to close it in favour of "realism", in the accepted, although quite indefensible, sense of that word. It is one thing, and true, to say that in cognition knowledge is claimed of a reality other than the cognitive event itself; it is quite another, and false, to say that the reality cognized in perception is necessarily a material-world-in-itself, or material objects-in-themselves. The stipulation that one's philosophical theory must recognize that cognition refers to an event beyond itself is fully satisfied *even by solipsism*! If I say "I alone exist, and my sensations refer to nothing outside me" I am as truly stipulating the existence of an entity *other than my present cognitive state* as I am if I postulate a material world. For I am affirming that a self persists in time and therefore transcends the affirmation-event itself. *A fortiori*, any non-solipsistic philosophy, whether realist or idealist, fully satisfies the requirement of recognizing that in cognition we "refer away" to an event beyond the cognitive event itself. The fact that a vase-percept implies a reality beyond itself is no proof that such reality is a vase-in-itself.

This brings us to a consideration of a type of criticism of idealism which is all too common but quite invalid. "The idealist", it is said, "regards cognition as a process in which a man is shut up to his own states. But this is absurd, for how can what goes on inside a man tell him anything about what goes on outside him? If our knowledge is knowledge of the real world, it must be a process in which we grasp or apprehend the real world direct."

In reply, let us notice that this argument derives its plausibility from the use of the metaphors "inside" and "outside", "grasp" or "apprehend". If we have a mental picture of a man as shut up inside a room, and if we think of cognition or knowledge as analogous to his grasping something with his hand, then, clearly, he can know, can touch or lay hold of, only such things as are in the room. But why use *any* metaphor for cognition or knowing? The knowledge-relation between knower and object known is *sui generis*. It is absurd to think that we can can "explain" it by using some analogy drawn from our picture of "the material world".

Now it is perfectly true that *in a sense* an act of cognition is a momentary event "within" a "mind"; it is personal and private. There *is* a sense in which each of us is "shut up to" his experiences. Apart from the extremely rare phenomenon of telepathy, which is probably to be regarded as a lingering survival from a lower evolutionary stage, our percepts and thoughts are as private as our toothache. From the standpoint of psychology they are separate events. The circle which I see is not the same as the ellipse which you see when we are seeing the alleged "same object". In one sense, then, the myth of the man-in-the-room is true. But in another sense it is not. It is not for us to "explain" how it is that what is in one sense a mental state of an ego can in another sense be knowledge *of* or knowledge *about* reality. We simply have to note the fact that knowledge is unique in exhibiting this particular kind of duality. There is nothing more inherently mysterious about this than there is about any other ultimate fact about the world—about the fact, for example, that the movement of a magnet inside my room in England can witness to the existence of a north pole far away. There is no contradiction between saying that we can know reality direct and saying that a cognition is a private event "in a mind". It is the peculiar characteristic of knowledge to be both. I simply have to accept the fact that the process of rendering my private thought-world consistent and coherent involves my postulating a reality transcending myself and my states to which my true judgments correspond. I interpret certain signs within my thought-world as evidence of an "external" William who has a pain. This kind of reasoning has not the theoretical certainty of deductive, i.e. logically necessary or tautologous reasoning. But it leads to practically or "morally" certain beliefs. In one sense I cannot transcend my own states—I cannot *be* anything or anyone other than what I am. But I can nevertheless *know that* other people exist.

In passing, let us notice that philosophers who have written about two theories of truth—the Coherence Theory and the Correspondence Theory, as though they were co-ordinate and mutually exclusive, have been mistaken. Consistency and coherence are the *tests* which I apply to my private thought-structure. But the structure which I approve because it is consistent and coherent with my experience may quite well include the notion of the existence of other persons and of God, and of correspondence between my true thoughts and a reality other than myself. In short, I can defend a theory of correspondence on the ground that it is consistent and coherent with itself and with my immediate experience. On what other grounds, incidentally, *could* I defend it?

I have insisted that the analysis of sentences the grammatical subjects of which are material-object nouns should be similar to that of sentences the grammatical subjects of which are words denoting personal qualities such as 'virtue'. But this is not to say that "the material world is unreal" or "does not exist". If it were contended that I regard the notion of the material world as an illusion, it would equally have to be contended that our analysis of sentences about virtue into sentences about virtuous people involves the belief that virtue is an illusion. To refuse to reify a noun, to insist that it is only a partial symbol in the sense explained on page 32 is one thing. To talk about the notion it stands for as unreal or illusory is quite another. People really are virtuous, and people really do perceive their percepts, as distinct from merely imagining them.

In a review in the *Sunday Times* of Viscount Samuel's book, *In Search of Reality*, Maurice Cranston criticized his dismissal of idealism as being too offhand. He quoted Lord Samuel as trying to refute idealism by writing: "If evidence is needed that the sun and its radiations really exist, a group of cattle on a hot summer afternoon, moving across the field to lie in the cool shade under the trees will give it." Mr. Cranston then commented as follows: "This pastoral scene proves nothing. No philosopher has ever been dotty enough to say that *only* the sun is unreal; idealists have questioned the reality of *all* material objects, and the reasons they have for denying the real existence of the sun would equally apply to fields and trees."

But the criticism is itself open to criticism. The statement that idealists question the reality of all material objects can give quite a wrong impression. I am tempted to say outright that idealists have *never* questioned the reality of the material world if the word 'reality' is given its common-sense meaning, and my only hesitation in saying this is that the word 'reality' *has* no one precise common-sense meaning. It has a variety of shades of meaning, but for my immediate purpose I wish to distinguish two broad but quite distinct senses in which it is used.

First, we say that something is real if it forces itself on us, makes us notice it—if we just *have* to take account of it. We say that a perceived fence is real whilst an imaginary fence is unreal. We can walk through the latter but we have to climb over the former if we wish to get to the other side. And objects which are real in this sense—those which have *material* reality—give us satisfactions which imaginary ones cannot. A real glass of water quenches my thirst; an imaginary one only aggravates it. But the word 'reality' covers more than material reality. We say that love is a reality, meaning that love forces us to take account of it, determines to a vast extent the course of human activity and gives us satisfaction. Philosophers, of course, have criticized the form of sentences of the type 'X is real', 'Y is unreal', quite rightly insisting that 'reality' is not an attribute; there are not two sorts of entities, real ones and unreal ones. But this does not concern us at the moment. We are concerned with popular usage.

But there is a second sense in which we use the word 'reality', and idealism results from an attempt to apply the test for reality in this sense consistently and persistently. The curious thing about this second sense is that the question whether we are to use the word 'real' or the word 'unreal' arises when the objective situation which we wish to characterize by one of these adjectives is unquestionably real in the first sense. I see a man across the road. In the first sense he is indubitably "real". But is my judgment "That is my friend Jones" a reality-judgment or does it express an illusion? It *looks*, let us say, like Jones. Why do I doubt it? Because I have good reason to believe that Jones is in Australia.

But why cannot I affirm that Jones is in Australia and is also in the Strand? Because Jones cannot *really* be both in Australia and in the Strand at the same time. He can only "appear to be", as we say. To the extent that an objective situation contains contradictions, it is only apparent, not real; we cannot be satisfied that we are talking about it correctly until we have a form of language which is free from self-contradictions. We are not, in popular parlance, seeing the world *as it really is* until we see it free from contradictions.

Closely connected with this sort of reality-judgment there is another. We do not feel that we are seeing the world as it really is if we see it as a heterogeneous hotch-potch of a variety of types of entities all existing side by side in glorious confusion. We insist that unless we can see some kind of connection, unity or system we are not seeing it "as it really is". I am not here concerned to criticize or justify this tendency of our thinking and speaking—this intellectual instinct. I am content to notice it, and to point out in passing that this instinct dominates our scientific thinking, which aims at connecting particular facts in wide generalizations, and that the triumphs of science are indication that we cannot dismiss the instinct as absurd.

Closely connected with this way of using the word 'real' is the tendency to deny the word 'real' to anything torn, so to speak, from the only context in which it is actually found. The absurdity of the idea that the whole of the cat could disappear and leave a bare grin is an instance of this, for we say "There couldn't be a grin without a grinner". We are, in effect, saying that an abstraction cannot really exist, cannot be real, without the concrete whole from which our thinking abstracts it. There are, then, two broadly contrasted senses in which we use the words 'real', 'reality' and 'really'. First, the test for 'reality' is that we shall be forced to take account of something "external" to us—something which does or could oppose our purposes, something which is sensed or felt and which gives us "real" satisfactions as opposed to something merely imagined. Second, we are knowing reality to the degree in which our knowledge is consistent, coherent and systematically unified, *and to the degree in which we explicitly notice the context in which alone an existent can exist and without which it is an abstraction.*

Now since we use the terms 'real' and 'unreal' in these two very different ways, we might well expect that all sorts of confusions and pseudo-problems would arise from failure to see and say exactly in which sense we are using the words. Our expectation is fully realized. The Christian Scientist may, or may not, be justified in characterizing pain and evil as unreal in the *second* sense: to discuss that would take us deeply into metaphysics. But it is absurd of him to expect us to agree to call pain unreal in the *first* sense merely because it may be unreal in the *second*. And certain idealists themselves are not free from blame for characterizing the material world as "unreal" without explicitly calling attention to what is implicit in their argument—that they are using the word in the second sense. But critics of idealism are the most to blame of all. For only bias or carelessness can prevent their seeing that thinkers of the calibre of Berkeley, Bradley or Bosanquet believed just as sincerely in the "reality" of the material world in the first, the most obvious, sense of the word, as does the crudest realist. The idealist is not denying the "reality" of the material world in the sense of its sensuous given-ness; he is merely denying a metaphysical theory about the material world—namely that it "really is" the isolated self-existent thing which the realist takes it to be. The idealist's insistence on subject-object polarity, his insistence that objects exist only for subjects, is quite compatible with his recognition of the difference between perception and imagination. It is one thing to say that the word 'object' should always be taken to mean 'object of cognition'. It would be quite another to say that the subject always approves of its objects —always wills their existence as objects.

It will now be clear that one of the tasks of the philosopher is to decide what nouns must be, and what nouns need not be, reified. Everyday language invites us to a *feast* of reification, and the philosopher must clearly exercise some austerity in the matter. It is clear that when two persons are discussing whether a noun should be reified or not, it would be absurd for either to expect the other to produce a *logically necessary* proof that the entity-in-question does or does not exist. The real problem is whether we *need* reify material-object-nouns, or whether we can analyse sentences in which they are grammatical subjects—'This table is hard'—as sentences about people's actual or possible percepts. The basic principle is that we do not reify unless we have to. I shall not defend this principle. A person who is prepared light-heartedly to reify any noun whatsoever is hardly likely to be reading this book. His world is a chaos, and if he is satisfied with it, there is nothing more to be said.

I need hardly point out that in treating the sentence 'This chair is heavy' as of the same type as 'Courage is valuable'— the same type in that they both require translation, for the purpose of philosophical analysis, into statements about people's experiences—I am taking a perfectly safe line. For I am not theorizing, not speculating; so far I am *refusing* to theorize or speculate. We all, without exception, agree that people have chair-percepts; we all agree that people are courageous. Very well, let us leave it at that, in *both* cases. I have no objection to using the form of statement 'This chair is heavy'; indeed, it would be very inconvenient to dispense with such language. But just as I decline to interpret 'Courage is valuable' as language about an objective courage-entity, so I decline to interpret 'The chair is heavy' as being about chair-in-itself. My refusal does not land me in self-contradiction, and, as we consider further objections, we shall see that it does not even land me in difficulties. Indeed, I shall show that it is the belief in chairs-in-themselves which lands one in difficulties. If I choose to define 'the existence of material objects' in terms of people's perceptual experience, I can get along quite nicely for ever. All statements of causal laws between "material objects" can be replaced by statements about regularities in the occurrences of people's percepts or about correlations between the respective perceptual experiences of different people.

But at the risk of being tedious I must reiterate that my reason for refusing to "take literally" language about a material world-in-itself, an objective time-in-itself or space-in-itself is not *merely* that there is not the slightest *need* to do so. There is, as I have shown, a positive reason for refusing to do so. We know that a person cognizes a spatially extended and temporally successive perceptual field. But the perception of an extended perceptual whole and the awareness of succession in time involve unity—unity-in-plurality—and the distinction between the plurality aspect and the unity aspect is the distinction between objects and subject. But are we prepared to say that plurality can exist apart from unity, and unity can exist apart from plurality? Are we prepared to regard plurality and unity as "things" in the literal sense? Plurality and unity are surely correlatives. The perceived objective whole, extended and changing, is therefore correlative to the *subject* of perception indicated by 'I', and it does not, therefore, make sense to talk about an extended and changing whole-*in-itself*—or to talk about space-*in-itself* and time-*in-itself*—i.e. to talk of them as if they could exist *as such* out of relation to the subject indicated by 'I'. The reservation "as such", is, of course, important. I am very far from suggesting that nothing objective is being cognized—that there is, in fact, no difference between perceiving something and imagining it. That there is something objective involved in perception which is not involved in mere imagination is clear. But the question at issue is in what language we are to describe this objective factor. All that I am contending for at the moment is that we must not over-simplify the problem by assuming that the objective factor is a material world-in-itself, existing in space-in-itself and changing in time-in-itself. Indeed, this book consists very largely of an attack on the whole notion of 'in itself'.

The reader may here ask whether I am seriously confining the meaning of "real existence" or "reality" to acts and contents of consciousness. Is there not, he may ask, a great deal more *in* the mind than is *before* the mind? Have not modern psychologists been forced to attach great importance to *unconscious* mental processes? In that case, why boggle at the notion of objects-in-themselves? The answer is simple. Suppose I fall asleep with a mathematical problem unsolved and awake to find the solution staring me in the face, does this prove that there is such a thing as unconscious thinking? Certainly not. It merely proves that the inferring process was no part of *my* consciousness. If it *was* really inference, then, since the only inferences of which we have any experience are inferences of conscious beings, we have no right to assume that language about *unconscious* inference has any meaning, and a more reasonable explanation is that I have been drawing on a super-Consciousness—an indwelling Mind to which all that to me is *potential* awareness is *actual* awareness. We shall arrive later at the notion of Reality as complete self-awareness, in contrast with that merely implicit or potential awareness characteristic of finitude.

My argument has not committed me to the view that language about the material world must, for philosophy, be replaced by language about a stream of sensations or sense-data or images. An individual perceives a world, and perceives it as continuous in time and space—no mere dance of sensa and images but a solid, resisting, very "real" world. But what I am insisting is that the world which Jones perceives is a *perceived* world, and it is *his* perceived world. "But this", you may say, "is a platitude. Indeed, it is worse, it is a tautology. *Of course* a world which is perceived is a perceived world, and *of course* if someone perceives a world it is perceived by him." And I accept this. But an important part of the philosopher's work is to make explicit what is implicit in platitudes and tautologies. In any case, it is less reprehensible to labour a tautology than to deny it!

One obvious difficulty with the alleged existence of material objects-in-themselves is to decide what is the "real" shape. Which of the percepts, Jones's or Smith's or Brown's, is or copies the "real" shape. In the case of simple objects such as a square sheet of metal, we tend to think of the person standing in front of it as having a privileged percept, as "seeing the thing as it really is". But this will not do; this test cannot be applied to irregularly shaped objects like a lump of rock. Does the latter then possess "in itself" all the shapes and sizes as seen by everyone who does see it or who could see it from all the possible directions and all the possible distances? Realists who are prepared at all costs to defend the notion of in-itself existence, and the notion that whatever we see exists in itself, just as we see it, and who honestly face the difficulties, have been led on to affirm that every material object is a set of "sensibilia" filling the whole of space. This does not escape my criticism of the error of reifying abstractions, but it shows the lengths to which we have to go if we try to defend the notion of objects-in-themselves. It shows that if we reject the idealist's construction on the ground that it conflicts with common sense we have, in the last resort, to adopt a view which conflicts with common sense just as much. Whatever the truth about the strange universe in which we live, it would certainly shock unreflective common sense if it could be stated clearly; there is not the slightest reason for questioning any philosophical construction on the ground of its strangeness.

You cannot escape the force of my argument by saying: "At least, there is one objective fact about the chair, which is the same for all observers. It has four legs." For what is this that is the same for all observers? Not a percept. The percept of four legs which Jones perceives is not the same as that which Smith perceives. The respective shapes are slightly or greatly different. They are different psychical entities; they exist in different fields. The common objective factor is the fact that the two percepts have a common feature, namely *fourness*. This is an additional justification for calling the perceptual object common to Smith and Jones an abstraction. First we called it an abstraction because it is, to use Bradley's language, torn from its context, its union with whatever 'I' stands for. And now we see it as an abstraction because it is the common feature, the resemblance, between the particular Smith-percept and the particular Jones-percept. Here, again, the common chair-in-itself is on a par with courage. The latter, too, is abstraction because first, it is torn from the egos which exhibit it, and secondly, it is the feature in which Smith's decision or action resembles Jones's.

3

OUR AWARENESS OF GOD

Our awareness of other people

A refusal to reify material-object-nouns involves one in the task of justifying one's willingness to reify person-names, i.e. one's refusal to be a solipsist and one's insistence that other people exist besides oneself.

But the task is quite simple. My refusal to reify material-object nouns was based on two facts. First, there is no *need* to do so. Second, there is a positive objection to doing so. Now neither of these two considerations holds in the case of personal nouns. There *is* a very real need to reify them, and there is not the slightest objection to doing so.

Let us take the second point first, for it can be stated very briefly. The objection to belief in objects-in-themselves was that it involved treating as a substance what is only an abstract aspect of the concrete unity of subject-with-object. But the assertion that other people exist does not involve this reification of an abstraction. It merely involves saying that if one subject-with-object exists, namely myself, other similar ones can exist too. This is quite valid. The objection therefore does not hold.

With regard to the *need* to reify person-names as compared with impersonal ones, the point is that in order to satisfy our

instinctive demand for a coherent account of our experience
—an account which does justice to all sides of that experience
—it is not in the least necessary to reify impersonal nouns but
it is absolutely necessary to reify personal ones. To insist, as I
do, that for philosophical analysis sentences with material-
object-nouns as grammatical subjects must be replaced by
sentences about people's experiences and actions leaves my
environment, and my reaction to it, practically unchanged.
For example, to refuse to reify impersonal nouns does not
prevent my helping realists to move the furniture or my play-
ing cricket with them. There is no practical, no psychological,
no moral, need to believe in material-objects-in-themselves.
But if I refuse to reify person-names, if I embrace solipsism, I
have to explain away—I cannot give a coherent account of—
my moral experience, my social instincts, my instinctive awareness of I-thou relationships. My consciousness of a duty to
others, my instinct to love and be loved—practically the whole
of those experiences which give life significance, would have
to be explained away.

Our awareness of God

We must now consider another objection. "So far", it may
be said, "you have tended to confine philosophy to analysis.
You have been concerned with the correct analysis of sentences with material-object-nouns as grammatical subjects.
You have taken the line that we ought not to reify nouns unless we have to, and you have argued that although we must
reify person-nouns we need not reify impersonal nouns. Now
I agree that we need not reify material-object-nouns in order
to operate successfully with sentences about material objects.
But surely, as rational beings, we have not only to operate
with such sentences; we need to be able to account for the fact

that we can correlate our respective perceptual worlds—as when we co-operate in moving the furniture. Do you dismiss this desire to account for this fact, on the ground that it involves us in metaphysical speculation? If so, are you consistent in postulating the existence of other people in order to account for your instinctive urges and for certain sensory experiences?"

My reply is simple. I am very far from questioning the legitimacy of our desire for, or our capacity for arriving at, speculative or metaphysical constructions which will in some sense "explain" or "account for" our perceptual experiences. I merely deny that the assertion of the independent existence of so-called material objects-in-themselves is the only, or the best, of such constructions.

What are the facts about percepts for which we as rational beings need to account? First, there is the obvious difference between perceiving and imagining; in practice we have no difficulty in distinguishing between feeling, seeing and tasting a real orange and merely imagining ourselves doing it. Second, a baby soon learns from experience that while his images have no counterpart in other people's experiences, his percepts do have such a counterpart. Thirdly, he soon finds that people can mutually co-ordinate and correlate their respective perceptual experiences; they can play games together, and so on. Now the obvious way for rational beings to account for these facts is to postulate that there is, metaphorically speaking, some objective factor "behind" our common perceptual experiences which is absent when one is indulging in private imaginings. This is common ground between so-called idealist and realist. Belief in this objective common ground is not a peculiarity of so-called realism. What is at issue is the *nature* of this common Something. Can we say anything about it, or must we just call it "The Unknowable"?

Now there is surely one thing that we can say with confidence, and our being able to say this entails that the factor we are discussing is not absolutely unknowable. We have seen grave objections to supposing that the object which exists independently of our perceiving it—the object which would be "there" if all finite beings became unconscious—is, or duplicates, any *abstract* feature of the concrete subject-object whole of experience. We must therefore believe that what we have been invited to call the Unknowable is at least as *concrete* as the subject-object *whole* itself. And we have seen that the one type of entity which we are all sure can and does exist "outside" ourselves is the conscious being who thinks and feels and chooses, an entity which is concrete in the sense of being a closely integrated unity of subject-with-object.

Now this is a proof that Objective Reality must, by rational beings, be conceived as analogous with Objective Mind and Will—must be conceived, that is, as not abstract object but concrete subject-with-object. I do not, of course, use the word 'proof' in the narrow sense of logically necessary or tautologous proof. But ordinary language, as we have noticed, very rarely does use it in that narrow sense. If we confine the word 'proof' to the sense of logically necessary proof we cannot, of course, prove that Objective Mind or God exists, but equally we cannot prove anything whatsoever about the real world— as modern logic has abundantly shown. In *that* narrow sense I cannot even prove that other people exist; I cannot even prove to myself that I exist as a continuous being who transcends the present momentary experience. But no sane person refrains from regarding all sorts of belief as certain, as "proved", merely because they are not expressed in tautologies. And I claim that the proof I have offered that Objective Reality is more adequately conceived as subject-with-object than as abstract object is as sound a proof as any constructive or non-tautological proof can be. It will not, of course, convince that person who, whether he admits it or not, does not want to be convinced. But unless there is this will to disbelieve it is sufficient.

The essential difference between perception and imagination is thus easily accounted for, without appealing to the existence of "matter", once we believe in Objective Mind and Will, i.e. in "God". We do not have to believe that an object ceases to be when finite beings cease to observe it. But the permanence and reality of the world are not a permanence and reality of a world "in itself"; the permanence and reality are "for God".

We have arrived at our belief in God in a curiously incidental way. We needed some account of perception other than the belief in matter, and belief in God presented itself as the obvious alternative. But to bring God in thus incidentally is not irreverent; indeed, it shows how inevitable God is for sound human thinking. We are not concerned with a distant God who long ago and once for all "created" a world and wound it up like a clock. God is One in whom we live and move and have our being.

To be freed from the bondage of a belief in dead "matter", to see the material world as Divine Object, which through the miracle of our being born can be also object to us, is ample reward for the sustained effort of close reasoning which we have had to make. We no longer feel ourselves alien intruders in a universe indifferent, if not hostile, to our hopes and aims. Reality is no longer a vastness compared with our littleness. We are both at the centre of Reality and also in some sense co-extensive with it. Our sense of beauty and of duty is no longer a subjective emotion repudiated by an "external reality" but a revelation of the God in whom we live and move and have our being. And, as we shall see, the sensuous world has become a symbolism of the spiritual world.

This is, indeed, the answer to anyone who belittles rational proofs of God's existence—anyone who, for example, tells us that a rational proof that what is behind the veil of sense must be referred to as "He" rather than "It" is of no value from the point of view of religion and of our everyday living. To decide that we must say 'He' rather than 'It' is of little importance *in itself*, but it is of infinite value because it opens up boundless possibilities. Our moral, aesthetic and religious experience can be rationally interpreted in one way if we believe that objective reality is analogous to subject-with-object—if we use the pronoun 'He'. But they must be interpreted quite otherwise if we regard reality as abstract, dead object and say 'It'. In the first case we can accept, and do full justice to, our conviction that our value-judgments express objective truth; for the good and the beautiful are taken to express the mind and will of God. In the second case we have to explain the conviction away. If there is no rational ground for believing in Personality beyond the veil of sense, then all those higher experiences which distinguish men from animals must be regarded as merely subjective feelings, irrelevant to and alien in a dead reality, and signifying precisely nothing beyond themselves. Those theologians who disparage the use of reason as a basis for Theism, and who appeal solely to mystical states or (as in the case of those theologians of "crisis" who disparage both reason and mysticism) to the experience of being "confronted" by God, have failed to see that in the act of saying *anything at all* about these experiences we are attempting a rational, i.e. a consistent and coherent construction, and that therefore there is no reason to interpret either of such types of experience as an experience of God unless there are *reasons* for believing in God. To interpret an immediate experience is to integrate it into our existing

63

thought-structure. The new data may, admittedly, modify the existing structure, but unless there is already at least an intellectual acquiescence in the idea of God, it is difficult to see how any immediate experience can, in its immediacy, create the idea. To be aware of a personality is a complex experience, involving *judgment*. One cannot have a pure *feeling* of the presence of another personality. One can have a sensation of redness or a feeling of joy or grief, but one cannot have a pure feeling of Jones—or of God—unmixed with thought.

It seems to me quite wrong to contrast reason with immediate experience as if they were alternative methods of coming to believe in God. There is *always* a rational element in religious belief. But constructive or inductive reason must have data to work on and these are supplied by experience and by history. Reason without experience would have no content. Experience without reason would have no form—would not be capable of statement in words at all.

4

TWO MAIN TYPES OF FACTUAL SENTENCE

We must now return to the point that what is described in the person-sentence 'I perceive a chair' is a closely integrated experience. The symbols 'I' and 'chair' do not describe separate entities which happen at the moment to stand in a relation accidental to their essential natures. On the contrary, these two symbols are *partial* symbols. No part of the sentence less than the whole stands for a concrete, isolated existent or event.

But can we claim that even the *whole* sentence stands for an entity or event existing or capable of existing by itself? Clearly not. What it stands for is more concrete, less abstract, richer in content than what 'I' or 'chair' stand for, but the event described by 'I am perceiving a chair' or 'William is perceiving a chair' or 'William is feeling a pain' is only one momentary phase in a series of phases which, as a series, has a unity. Personal nouns like 'William', when they occur in such a sentence, have no more claim to stand for entities than do the word-symbols 'I' and 'chair'. 'William' functions in the same way as does 'I'. Just as the symbol 'I', when I use it, does not stand for a separate entity but indicates the unity of *my* conscious life, so the word 'William', when I use it, indicates the unity of *his* conscious life. The symbol 'William', when used in this way, indicates a unity which has two aspects. It indicates the unity of his consciousness *at any moment*, and also the unity conferred on what would otherwise be a succession in time of separate mental happenings by the fact that they constitute one memory-chain—one person's "inner life", as we say, continuing over a period of time. To represent the William-entity *fully* one would need the *totality* of sentences, each with 'William' as grammatical subject, forming a running commentary on his thoughts and feelings and actions from birth. These sentences would form one class in virtue of the fact that each contained the word 'William' as grammatical subject, but the fact remains that *in each sentence* the word 'William' would be but a partial or abstract symbol. Of course we can, if we choose, use the word 'William' all by itself, i.e. not in a sentence, and say that we intend it to have the same objective reference as has the concrete *totality* of the William-sentences. But this would be quite a different symbol from 'William' as used *in* the sentences; we might write it 'WILLIAM'.

We now come to a point of great importance. We have seen that there are two different types of factual sentence. On the one hand there are *personal* sentences, by which I mean sentences to the effect that conscious beings are experiencing something or are choosing or willing or acting. On the other hand there are impersonal sentences, by which I mean sentences the grammatical subjects of which are material-object or scientific phrases or nouns such as 'The table' or 'Electrons' or 'Waves' or are abstract nouns or phrases such as 'Virtue' or 'To travel hopefully'. Now when we believe that the sentence 'William feels a pain' is true, we believe that the sentence stands in a very simple relation of correspondence to a momentary phase of the William-continuum referred to in the preceding paragraph. Indeed, we should probably, if asked, explain our affirmation of the truth of the sentence by saying "I mean there *really is* a William who *really is* feeling a pain". But when we say "Unpunctuality is reprehensible" we do not believe that this same simple relation holds between the sentence and what it stands for; we do not believe that there is an unpunctuality-entity possessing the quality of reprehensibility in the same way that there is a William possessing the quality of being pained. And, as my preceding argument has proved, there is no reason to believe, and serious difficulties in believing, that the objective situation described by 'This vase is green' is a vase-entity-in-itself possessing in itself the quality of being green. *In short, we cannot claim that true impersonal language corresponds to reality with that simple directness which true personal language achieves.* For philosophical analysis, whether regarded as an end in itself or as a preliminary to philosophical construction or metaphysics, impersonal language must be translated into personal language.

Our ordinary or everyday language is, of course, a mixture of both these main types of language, and I shall have little difficulty in showing that this practically convenient, though philosophically illegitimate, mixture of two different languages and this merging of two separate language-standpoints has been metaphysically muddling, and has led to a number of pseudo-problems. Personal language rightly reifies personal nouns and impersonal language wrongly reifies a whole host of impersonal nouns, and the effect on popular metaphysics of the consequent assumption that "minds" exist alongside of these other types of entity in one and the same "world", has been philosophically disastrous. For example, there is the pseudo-problem of seeing how the alleged chair-in-itself is objectively related, causally or otherwise, to someone's chair-percept. Once we have faced the obvious fact that personal language and impersonal language are related to reality in quite different ways, it is clear that the notion that all nouns whatsoever stand for co-ordinate entities jostling one another in one and the same objective continuum is nonsense. I shall return to this point later, but before doing so I must consider a further objection to my main argument, and then call attention to the support which that argument has received from modern physics.

Idealism and common sense

"You have", it may be said, "skated too lightly over important differences between the two cases which you have treated as similar. To treat courage or unpunctuality as substances is, admittedly, only a convenient linguistic device, but language about material entities can have a precision which language about personal qualities has not. It is not merely a question of saying vaguely 'There is a material world'. The relationship between what various people perceive can be given an exact mathematical formulation. Indeed, one person can calculate what another person *must* be perceiving if his eyes are open."

My answer is this. To say that the two cases are essentially similar is not to deny their very real differences. I do most emphatically affirm that a perceived world is as much an abstraction from the concrete event I-am-perceiving-a-perceived world as is pain from I-am feeling-a-pain, but I do not deny the obvious differences between the two. The sensory or perceptual abstraction is, because of its spatial character, capable of a detailed mathematical treatment which is impossible in the case of emotions, personal qualities and volitions. All that I wish to maintain is that when we say that

Jones's percept and Brown's percept at this moment are "percepts of one and the same table from different angles" the analysis of this phrase and the test of its truth must, in the nature of things, be in terms of *the precepts themselves*. First consider the perceived objects in my own perceptual field. How do I decide that this patch of colour in one part of my visual field is "the same as" a similar patch which a few moments ago was in another part of that field? The tests for sameness must, in the nature of things, be tests applicable to *what is actually seen*. I do not "transcend" or "go behind" what I actually see. And the same is true when two persons decide that they are perceiving "the same object". To say that Jones and I are perceiving the same object is a way of telling me how a certain percept in my perceptual field would change its shape and position if my field were to become exactly similar to Jones's. Even if our discussion involved mathematics this could be interpreted *without introducing the notion of a material world-in-itself*.

It is often assumed by metaphysical realists that they have common sense on their side. Even if this is true, it is not impressive; common sense in its cruder forms is not infallible. Nor is it possible to draw a sharp line between common sense and philosophy. Philosophy is only common sense applied with patient thoroughness. But my immediate object is to question the assumption that common sense even in its cruder forms is always realistic without qualms. The truth is that crude common sense is muddled, and it is because it is dimly aware of this that it is driven on to philosophy. If you ask the plain man whether the table remains in the empty room when no one is there to see it, he replies "Of course it does". But this is not realism in the metaphysical sense. For if you suggest to him that what he *means* is that anyone who goes into the room can see and feel the table, he will probably reply "Good

69

enough" and wonder what all the fuss is about. It is as true of metaphysical idealism as of metaphysical realism that it has roots in common sense.

From my own experience I should say that the qualms about metaphysical realism are often felt quite early in life. I have a vivid recollection of sitting in school and gazing dreamily at one of the four pillars which supported the roof and feeling vaguely that there was some kind of problem in the fact that in some sense the pillar existed and yet was unconscious. After all, our notion of existence has been abstracted from experience—from conscious existence. Can we have the least confidence that the notion of a non-experienced and non-experiencing existent is a valid one?

5

SCIENCE AND IDEALISM

The foregoing analysis of sentences about so-called "material objects" was not occasioned by any modern scientific theory or experiment. Indeed, it obviously goes back to Berkeley who lived long before the Newtonian theory of the world was challenged by the scientists. But our analysis does happen to be supported from the discovery of the facts which led to the Special Theory of Relativity.[1] For not only are those facts difficult to fit into a belief in a three-dimensional world-in-itself in a common or public time, but they can be given a mathematical interpretation of beautiful simplicity if we give up this notion of common or public time and space measurements and allow that such measurements are always "for" an observer. This means that an object cannot be said to have length "in itself" and an interval cannot be said to have duration "in itself". We can speak significantly of length only if we mention the observers of length. The respective lengths, for different observers, of what everyday language calls "the same object", are not correlated in the simple way

---

[1] The results of the Michelson-Morley experiment have received confirmation in an experiment by Dr. Essen of the National Physical Laboratory, using not light-waves but short-length radio-waves. See *Nature*, 7th May 1955.

which the naïvely realistic concept of a common "material-object-in-itself" demands; the correlation is much more complicated. And similar considerations apply to the case of time-intervals. Indeed, in certain circumstances it is not significant to say that event A precedes event B. For in these circumstances, the Special Theory demands that one type of observer would see A preceding B while another would see B preceding A. It would be meaningless to ask which was the "true" time-order—the order of time-in-itself, for there is no time-in-itself.

There was, of course, even in days when Newton's picture of a world-in-itself in a common or public space-in-itself and a common or public time-in-itself was generally accepted, a sense in which space and time intervals were "relative to an observer". The same object would look big to one observer—it would almost fill his visual field—while looking small to another, i.e. filling only a small part of his visual field. And the "same" time interval would "pass" more quickly for an interested than for a bored person. Moreover the time-interval as measured by one scientist might appear different from that measured by another because allowance had not been made for the time taken by the light wave. But relativities of this kind could easily be explained on the old view; they left intact the old theory of a common world in a common time and a common space. But the Michelson-Morley experiment led to a much more radical relativism. According to the Special Relativity Theory, space and time intervals are *essentially* relative to an observer. There *is* no time-in-itself and space-in-itself. This insistence on reference to an observer fits beautifully into the view of the Universe which I have advocated— the view of it as a system of conscious beings with private perceptual fields inter-related in some way far more subtle and complex than by being caused by a three-dimensional world-in-itself in a common time-in-itself and space-in-itself.

The idealistic implications of the Special Theory of Relativity would have been generally recognized were it not that when the Theory became known to the general public in 1919, there had begun that reaction against the late-Victorian and Edwardian idealism which has only recently begun to show signs of weakening. As it was, philosophers were only too ready to appeal to Minkowski's more or less pictorial "interpretation" of the new mathematics—a four-dimensional space-time continuum—and therefore to assume that the idea of a world-in-itself had not been challenged. They were encouraged in this by the fact that Einstein himself did not claim that his theory supported idealism—a fact which should not have weighed with them, since pre-eminence in physics does not imply any special authority in philosophy. Now the interpretation by imaginative pictures of *any* mathematics used by observers in the mutual correlation of their respective sense-experiences or private worlds is a matter of practical convenience and not of logical necessity. (This applies also to such scientific pictures as electrons, waves and energy.) We have seen that there is no reason to take literally language about "the" three-dimensional material world—language which common sense quite naturally used to interpret the Newtonian mathematics. We saw no reason to regard the block-universe as an independent entity existing in itself. Now all the objections to taking literally the *old* picture of a common world—objections to regarding it as anything more than a useful "as-if" device—clearly apply to the suggestion that we must take the *new* Minkowski picture literally. But in addition there is a further one.

The idealist's treatment of the old three-dimensional material world is, admittedly, at first sight a little shocking, although when one becomes accustomed to it it ceases to shock. But there is nothing in the least shocking in the suggestion that the picture which modern science has had to substitute for the old three-dimensional world *is* merely a picture and not a thing-in-itself. For it is a picture of a four-dimensional space-time world measured by "complex numbers", which are artificial, although quite logical, constructions. Strictly speaking, it is not even a "picture", for we cannot visualize a four-dimensional space, still less visualize lengths measured by complex numbers. The interpretation of mathematical variables by "dimensions" is, in fact, a game which must not be taken seriously. One's common sense is surely far more affronted by the suggestion that this four-dimensional "picture" is a self-existent entity than by the suggestion that it is merely a device which we find useful in the co-ordination of our sense-experience and for practical co-operation. One of the axes in this four-dimensional continuum is a time axis, and all movement or change is therefore frozen, so to speak, as surely as it is in a railway time-table. But in saying that this continuum is changeless we must be careful to guard against the natural tendency to picture this changelessness as a persistence unchanged *in time*. A four-dimensional space-time continuum is neither spread out in space nor persistent in time. In this respect the words 'space-time continuum' resemble the abstract words 'virtue' and 'unpunctuality', and we are thus brought back to the point that there is no more need to postulate the objective existence of our four-dimensional world than to postulate the objective existence of a virtue-entity. Just as we can cover all the facts about virtue by talking about people who are, and do, good, so we can cover all the facts about the alleged four-dimensional entity by talking about what is seen by observers in their three-dimensional privately-sensed worlds and about what devices—whether "pictures" or mathematical equations

—they use for correlating these worlds. It is difficult to imagine a clearer vindication of the philosophical analysis which leads to the insistence on person-language as alone philosophically accurate than the discovery of the facts which led to the Special Theory of Relativity.

In discussing relativity I have confined myself to the Michelson-Morley experiment and to the Special Theory which so beautifully accounts for the results of that experiment. I have not thought it necessary to refer to the General Theory or to the cosmological theories of Eddington or Milne or Hoyle. For from the point of view of the philosophy I am expounding scientific cosmology has no great philosophical importance—as I shall later point out. Moreover, no cosmological theory can afford to ignore the results of the Michelson-Morley experiment or can detract from the impressiveness of the fact that the simplest "explanation" of the results of that experiment involves, in effect, the denial of the existence "in themselves" of a space-order and a time-order. It is this consideration which doubtless led Eddington, when Einstein indulged in later cosmological speculations which envisaged an "absolute" space and time for the Universe as a Whole, to offer the following comments "Just as each limited observer has his own particular separation of space and time so a being co-extensive with the world might well have a special separation of space and time natural to him. It is time for this being that is here dignified by the title of 'absolute'."[1] Even, then, if the concept of an ultimately absolute time and space were clearly demanded by the results of any experiment—and I understand that this is not the case—this "absoluteness" must be explained as the Divine awareness.

But it is not only the relativity-theory of large-scale and

[1] See G. J. Whitrow. *The Structure of the Universe.* (Hutchinson.) Page 79.

75

astronomical physics that forces us, in effect, to interpret language about "the physical universe" as language about the observations of observers, and to regard our mental pictures of objects-in-themselves as helpful but not essential "interpretations" of mathematics. For the same is true of atomic physics. For one thing, the Special Theory of Relativity was found to accord remarkably well with the results of experiments in atomic physics, and for another, it was found that we cannot get just one clear and consistent picture in three-dimensional space of the working of the atom and the transmission of energy which can be used to illustrate *all* the equations. Different equations need different pictures, and these pictures are not consistent with each other. We have a choice between a wave-picture and a particle or energy-bundle picture, and this fact strongly supports our contention that our pictures of objects-in-themselves, while useful devices for enabling us to anticipate and control the course of our sensory experience, must not be thought of as corresponding in a simple way to, or being copies of, "external" objects-in-themselves. It is perfectly safe to say that if men had not got into the metaphysically objectionable habit of regarding the Newtonian world-picture as the picture of a self-existent, independent world-in-itself, they would not have had the least temptation to regard the interpretative pictures of *modern* physical equations as anything more than useful fictions or "as if" illustrations. It is ridiculous to claim the support of common sense for a "realistic" belief in a world-in-itself now that common sense is no longer able to believe in the *Newtonian* world-in-itself.

It is always possible, of course, that some scientist will one day succeed in getting one consistent "model" which will illustrate all the equations. This, however, would *not* be an experimental verification of metaphysical realism. For the idealist analysis was first made when the Newtonian world-picture was unchallenged. That analysis does not *need* the support of modern physics, and it would not be falsified even if the Newtonian picture were reinstated. But in view of the results of the Michelson-Morley experiment it is far from likely that even if a single model could be constructed which would serve to illustrate or interpret all the equations used in atomic physics, relativity theory and cosmogony, it would be of such a simple character that we could easily think of it as a thing-in-itself. My criticisms of the notion that the Minkowski world is a thing-in-itself are relevant here, and the model in question would presumably be far more complex than that. A model with a number of dimensions greater than three, or a model measured by complex numbers, or a model in which one axis is a time-axis and in which time is therefore "frozen", cannot be claimed as *obviously* a thing-in-itself, as realists used to claim that the Newtonian world was.

Some scientific writers have suggested that the question whether entities can be affirmed to exist or not is meaningless. I should agree that for physical science the question need not arise, and is, therefore, for such science, meaningless. But for philosophy the question is not meaningless, for language which suggests that material particles have existence in themselves is "systematically misleading", to borrow a phrase coined by Professor Gilbert Ryle. For such language suggests, as we shall see, misleading metaphysical propositions, such as that our "bodily" processes are "the cause" of our mental ones, and that men are small—with the suggestion that they are therefore insignificant—in comparison with the alleged vastness of this mythical Universe-in-itself.

It is relevant here to call attention to the work on parapsychology carried out by Professor Rhine of Duke University, U.S.A., and by Dr. Soal and others under the auspices of

77

the Society for Psychical Research—to say nothing of the most impressive records of spontaneous psychical manifestations collected by that society. It is easy to understand the hostility aroused in certain scientific quarters towards the claim that such phenomena as clairvoyance, telepathy or prevision had been scientifically demonstrated, for on the hypothesis that a three-dimensional block-universe of energy and matter is in some sense a basic reality and that mental events are by-products of physical ones, the occurrence of such phenomena appears impossible. But from the standpoint which I am advocating such phenomena are no more surprising than any others. The evidence for them is, in fact, very strong.

6

LANGUAGE ABOUT "BODIES" AND "MINDS"

Our analysis of language about material objects is of vital importance for the interpretation of statements about the relation between our so-called "bodies" and "minds". For the analysis clearly applies as much to those material objects which we call "bodily organisms" as to inorganic bodies. Language about my body should, like language about my chair, be translated, as a preliminary to philosophical construction, into language about what is, or will be, or may be sensed or perceived in certain people's and my own fields of consciousness.

Let us consider the whole event symbolized by the sentence 'He perceives a patch of colour'. Since the symbol 'He perceives' and the symbol 'patch of colour' do not stand for separate entities, but stand for abstractions from the whole event, it would clearly be absurd to talk about the perceiving being "caused" by the patch of colour—as absurd as saying that north is caused by south or that the shape of a vase is caused by its matter. And the absurdity of regarding what 'he' stands for, or what 'he perceives' stands for, as *caused* by what 'a patch' stands for remains not only when the seen patch is what everyday language calls a bit of someone else's body but also when it is a bit of the percipient's own body.

Now to say that Jones has a body is to say that his existence as a conscious being, and in some measure his thoughts and emotions, are made known to other people by percepts in their fields of consciousness. (This needs supplementing by pointing out that in addition to Jones's direct and immediate knowledge of his own thoughts and emotions he has also a perceptual awareness of himself similar to Smith's awareness of him; he can see his own frown in the looking-glass.) Language, therefore, about Jones's body should, before we begin philosophical construction, be translated into language about percepts in Smith's, Brown's and Jones's own fields of consciousness or private worlds. We thus avoid the absurd notion of two separate "realms"—a "physical" and a "mental" with a gulf between, over which causal activities take place. All so-called body-mind "interaction" can with perfect adequacy (although, of course, with far less practical convenience) be described in personal language, i.e. in sentences the grammatical subjects of which indicate conscious beings and the verbs and grammatical objects of which indicate perceivings of and thinkings about percepts.

This result is absolutely final and irrefutable. The point at issue is a purely philosophical one. No discovery in the field of physiological psychology could possibly invalidate it, for, as we have seen, the body-mind language in which the physiological pyschologist might quite reasonably prefer to state it must, in the nature of things, be translatable into personal language, and, equally in the nature of things, no evidence that the translation is inadequate can be produced. The Universe can with perfect adequacy be described as a society of conscious beings. Within each being can be distinguished, not as separate entities, but as abstract aspects, the unity of awareness or "the ego", percepts, thought-constructions, emotions, volitions. Changes in one person's percepts are normally accompanied by changes in certain other persons' percepts. (For example, they see "the same moving object".) We can describe this general fact as due to there being a *pre-established harmony* between individuals' perceptual fields. This phrase, when we are confining ourselves to analysis and refraining from philosophical construction, merely records an obvious fact and does not indicate any particular way of accounting for the harmony. My immediate point is that if we wish to be completely cautious, if we wish to state all causal "laws" in terms which avoid speculative constructions, realist or idealist, we must state them as correlations between percepts in a perceptual field—as when the felt pressing of the seen switch is followed by a seen light—or as correlations between two separate fields, as when my moving of an object causes you to see a movement also.

In rejecting the notion of causal laws operating over a gulf between two separate "realms", a physical and a mental, it is important to avoid a possible misunderstanding. I am not contending that there is anything inherently impossible in the notion that a cause can operate between two "things" as disparate as a "body" and a "mind". Our statements of causal laws are merely generalized statements of observed regularities of sequence. We cannot say in advance what sequences are possible or impossible; no sequence is inherently more "understandable" than any other, although we tend to think it is because it is more familiar. It is only because I reject the notion of two separate realms that I reject the notion of causes operating between them.

The existence of each conscious being, and the nature of his thoughts, emotions and volitions, are signalled to other conscious beings by ever-changing body-percepts cognized by the latter. We learn to interpret these signs by experience, but there is, I suggest, evidence that infants, and even adults, do so to some extent instinctively. Over many of these percepts the conscious being to whose existence and states they testify has no control; in everyday language we "cannot help being seen" by other people. Over others we have conscious control; we can smile voluntarily and we can tell people our thoughts, i.e. we can initiate changes in our, and thus in their, sense-experiences. All the various situations which in everyday language we describe in terms of actions and reactions between a thing-in-itself body and the mind or mental processes of the possessor of that body, or between someone's body and other people's minds or mental processes, can be translated, and ought to be translated when we are philosophizing, into person-language, i.e. language about the relations between events or percepts in one person's experience or about relations between one person's and another person's experience.

Let us now examine one or two instances of the sort of translation I have in mind. Take the instance where, in ordinary language, one person "tells another his thoughts". There is here a relation between sounds and bodily sensations experienced (and, of course, initiated) by the first person, and sounds in the second person's consciousness which the latter has learned to interpret. Or take the case where one person reads amusement or love in the "look" given him by another; the first person is interpreting some of his percepts—percepts which are part of the stuff of his own being—as symbolizing the existence and emotional life of another person.

An important case is where one person claims to assess the mentality of another by observing the shape of his skull. A doctor, for example, may prophesy that a new-born infant will grow up mentally deficient, or a phrenologist may tell us that he will be musical. Assuming that these prophecies are justified, we must not say that the structure of the skull causes the later psychological events—events in the child's "mind". This is to fall into error of postulating two separate realms, a physical or material and a mental, which act and react causally on each other. All that we have a right to say is that the doctor or phrenologist has had certain percepts which he is justified as regarding as signs of some existing psychological conditions in the child which will tend to issue in deficient mental functioning or in musical experiences. The "shape of the skull" is a percept which exists only in a person's sense-field, and this particular kind of percept normally exists only in the fields of persons other than the person whom everyday language calls "the owner of the skull". The skull percept, then, is not a cause of anything in the child's psychological make-up; it is only a cause in the experience of the owner of the perceptual field to which it belongs, in this case the doctor or the phrenologist. It is a cause in the sense that it causes him to prophesy.

Now in reply to my insistence that this translation of body-mind language into what I have called personal language is perfectly adequate and irrefutable, the reader may urge that the point is of merely linguistic and not of material importance. "The fact still remains" it may be said, "that one person can affect another's mental processes. One person can hurt another physically, can make him drunk or can inject drugs into him. You can say, if you like, and I cannot refute you, that language about Jones's body should be translated into language about the sensuous or perceptual signs or symbols of Jones in other people's consciousnesses, but you must admit that these sensuous signs or symbols are quite different in one vital respect from any other kind of sign or symbol. For example, the written word 'Jones' on a piece of paper is a symbol of Jones, but I can tear up or burn the paper without injuring Jones. But if I punch the Jones-face-symbol in my field of consciousness, Jones feels a pain."

My reply is simple. *Of course* the symbols are unique. We have to make the word 'symbol' cover a variety of cases. But the use of the term is justified; the percepts which I call the percepts of Jones's body in my own field of consciousness do signify to me Jones's existence and inner states, in somewhat the same way as do marks on a piece of paper. But there is no inconsistency between using the term 'symbol' and noticing the fact that I can hurt Jones by acting on my Jones-percept. And with regard to your point that our choice of language does not affect the facts, again I agree. So far as science and everyday life are concerned it makes no difference whether we use the body-mind language or the purely personal language. My only reason for labouring the point that the personal language is more *philosophically* accurate is that the body-mind language suggests to our minds a false metaphysic. Body-mind language is "systematically misleading". It suggests, that is, that a man consists of a body which is an entity-in-itself, and that his consciousness is a sort of by-product. And if one revolts against this as obviously unsatisfactory, but is still metaphysically under the influence of the body-mind language, one thinks of a "spirit" as living inside the body like a dog in a kennel or of thoughts and memories as being inside a brain-box. And one is then more or less bound either to deny the possibility that our personalities can survive the destruction of our bodies, or else to postulate a "disembodied" existence after death—a notion which raises acute difficulty if indeed it is not completely unintelligible, and which, moreover, suggests a dreary conception of the hereafter—very different from the Christian conception of *embodied* existence.

The body-mind language suggests moreover, a too rigid

distinction between perceiving and imagining. It suggests, that is, that there is the process of perceiving just the one "real" (i.e. material) world, on the one hand, and that there is to be set against this, on the other hand, only that process of perceiving "what is not there" which we call imagination. It ignores the possibility that there might be "material worlds" which might be visible to some but not all. For the term "*the* material world" certainly *suggests* that there can only be one, and it is only when we face the fact that language about the material world is translatable into language about pre-established harmony between perceptual worlds that there opens before us the very real possibility that there may be a number of such harmonies, each of which holds as between the perceptual fields of only a limited number of people. That this is not merely a wild possibility is certainly suggested by the considerable evidence for the phenomenon of collective hallucination—where two or more people see the same "apparition". You cannot dispose of this by saying that one person's imagination telepathically influences the imaginations of others, for if such telepathic influences are thorough enough and permanent enough you have, in every sense, a "material world". Suppose, for example, that ten persons share in a collective hallucination—a system of pre-established harmony—*for a long period.* Can you deny that they are perceiving a "real" world? Suppose for ten you substitute a thousand, and suppose the "hallucination" goes on for three score years and ten. On what grounds can you deny reality?

It is clear, then, that my insistence that body-mind language must be translated into personal language is no *mere* question of language. To say that language about our "bodies" must be interpreted as language about perceptual signs of our existence as conscious beings carries certain ontological implications. It pre-supposes, in fact, what might be called an *inverted* epiphenomenalism. The epiphenomenalistic view of body-mind relations which characterized scientific material-ism was that the body was the obvious reality, and that the mind was in some way "derived", and in saying this one was influenced by some such analogy as that of the candle (the body) to its flame (the mind). The view which I am advocat-ing, whilst agreeing with it in being monistic—in rejecting a dualism of co-ordinate and interacting entities, body and spirit —reverses the direction of the dependence. The basic realities from which our thinking must begin are conscious beings. Sensing and thinking and having emotions—these are pro-cesses which are most certainly going on and which cannot be "reduced" to anything other than themselves. It is *these* that can be likened to the candle, and it is the sensory signs, the body-appearances, that can be likened to the flame. This con-clusion carries an obvious implication which is certainly far more than verbal, namely that all arguments to the effect that human personalities cannot survive the deaths of their bodies since the former are epiphenomena of the latter, are invalid. The question of survival is—if we leave religious faith out of the discussion—a purely empirical one. Survival is at the lowest a very real possibility. The death of the body merely means the cessation of the possibility of using one particular class of signs or symbols. The possibility that after death other sorts may be available becomes a very real one. Moreover, we are no longer confronted by the antithesis between "one real material world" on the one hand and disembodied spirits on the other hand indulging in mere remembrance of that one world and in mere imagination. There is the very real possi-bility that there could be limited groups of conscious beings between whose sensory experiences there existed a pre-estab-lished harmony or who, in other words, experienced a common world unperceivable by others. This would mean not merely the metaphysical conceivability of "heaven" but of "many mansions" (to quote the fourth gospel).

It would be tedious, and unnecessary, to give examples of the type of language-translation I am advocating. Quite obviously it would cover cases of the psychological effects of drug-injections or of gland-deficiencies; in all cases the causal relation could be stated as a relation between perceivings, feelings, volitions, in the consciousness of one person, or as a relation between the perceivings, etc., of different people. But it is necessary to reply to an objection which may possibly arise in some reader's mind. He may say: "But you are substituting for an easily understood type of causal relation a fantastic one. That a blow on a physical organism causes pain is easily understood, but that a person's initiation of sensory changes in his own sense-field should be described as the cause of a second person's feeling pain is fantastic." The answer is simple. The objection falls to the ground because it pre-supposes that we can see that some causal sequences are *inherently* reasonable or intelligible; it presupposes that we can see not only that event A causes event B but also *why* event A causes event B. Now every scientist and every philosopher knows that this is false. Causal laws are merely statements of observed regularities, and in the final analysis no type of causal law is, *for human thinkers,* more reasonable or explicable than any other. The only way in which human beings can achieve knowledge of causal laws is by observation or experiment. Statements about causal regularities of sequence between people's experiencings are, therefore, quite as satisfactory as are statements to the effect that causal relations hold between alleged "bodily" and "mental" states. The latter language is not more intelligible, it is merely more familiar. And the former language has the advantage of keeping more closely

87

to what is observed and avoiding the unnecessary reification of nouns.

Another objection must be dealt with here. The objector may, indeed he must, concede that a causal law in body-mind terms is no more ultimately intelligible than one in terms of people's perceivings. But he may point out that the former type of law is far more practically useful. By conceiving such things as atoms and light-waves and energy particles we have been able to build up the sciences of chemistry and physics, the researches of which are carried on in impersonal language. Moreover, although we can quite adequately talk about the events leading up to and following the experience of pain in purely personal language, the fact remains that the business of applying science to the cure of disease and the relief of pain has been greatly facilitated by that very body-mind language which from the standpoint of philosophy I have rejected.

Now this objection is apparent, not real. It actually supports our analysis. For it brings us to the point that the function of impersonal language, suggesting as it does mental pictures of material objects-in-themselves, is not to mirror objective reality in any simple way but to achieve practical results—to show us for example how to obtain the sensory experiences we desire (such as the cessation of pain). I am very far from saying that impersonal language has no function and should not be used. My only concern is to compare the respective functions of person-language (i.e. language in terms of persons' experiencings of their private worlds) and impersonal language (i.e. language about "the" material world, material objects, scientific objects like electrons and energy, and abstract qualities). I will deal with this in the next section.

7

THE ERROR OF MIXING PERSONAL
AND IMPERSONAL LANGUAGE

The most vital difference between the two languages lies in the conception of *truth* appropriate to each. If an educated person is asked what is meant by the "truth" of a statement, he will almost certainly reply somewhat to the effect that a true statement is one which corresponds to the reality of the situation to which it refers. His essential idea is that the true statement *corresponds*. There is something objective, and the truth or falsity of the statement is a relation between the statement and this objective reality.

Now if we accept this definition of truth, and if we concern ourselves only with what we *mean* by "truth" and not with the methods whereby we *test* statements for truth, we can see that it applies to personal statements without difficulty. If I say "William is feeling a pain" or "William is angry", then, assuming that I believe what I am saying, I hold that there really exists objectively a William who really is feeling pain or who really is angry. But, as we have noticed, when we say "Silence is golden" we do not believe that there is a silence-entity which possesses objectively the attribute of being golden, and my preceding discussion has shown that words like 'table', 'energy', 'the material world', and so on, resemble 'silence' in not standing for entities-in-themselves when they are used as grammatical subjects of sentences. These sentences, *as a whole*, are true *of an objective situation* when they are true at all, but they do not correspond to that situation in the simple direct way in which *personal* sentences correspond. We cannot, in the case of these impersonal sentences, claim that there is an objective entity corresponding to the grammatical subject-noun, and a simple objective quality corresponding to the object-adjective. The value of true impersonal sentences lies in their facilitating mental processes which enable us to anticipate sense-experiences, react to them and co-ordinate our actions in our perceived worlds with those of our fellows in theirs. The scientist regards statements about electrons, energy, etc., as being true if they can be verified—i.e. if they lead him correctly to anticipate the nature of some sense-experience, and as false if experience disappoints the expectation based on them. Similarly, the sentence 'This piece of iron is hot' is regarded as true if, on touching the iron, we receive a sensation of heat.

The conception of truth appropriate to personal language s thus different from that appropriate to impersonal language. In the former case it is of the greatest importance to distinguish the *meaning* of 'truth' from the *test* for truth, but in the latter case, although this distinction, of course, still holds, it is of little importance to insist on it. For example, I can test my belief that William is angry by making a remark which induces him to throw a book at me, but when I say "William is angry" it is of the utmost philosophical importance to insist that I am not merely making an elliptical remark about the possibility of books being thrown. The whole of morality and religion and, indeed, the escape from solipsism itself, is involved in the distinction. But when I am asked what I mean when I say that the statement 'Arsenic is poisonous' is true, it is of little value, although correct, to say that the objective situation is different from what it would be if the statement were false. The only really useful thing I can say is to point to the ways in which the statement has been verified. The logical positivists were going too far in *defining* 'meaning' and 'truth' in terms of verification, but they are perfectly right, so far as impersonal sentences are concerned, in insisting that the only question of any importance which arises when we discuss the truth of impersonal sentences is that of the way of falsifying or verifying them.

The impersonal sentences of physics have by some writers been called fictions. There is no objection to this term so long as it is not taken to connote falsity, and it can be applied to all impersonal sentences. Fictional language can be true or false. To say 'The fiction A is true' is to say that it will be a correct guide to future experience. And since, in the case of true fictions, our future experience will be the same as it would be if the fictional entities really existed, fictional language can quite appropriately be described as "as if" language.

We now come to a point of the utmost importance. Since the functions of the two types of language—personal and impersonal language—are so different, and since they are related to reality in different ways, the one direct and simple and the other indirect and complex, we must expect to find that the mixing of the two languages, in the way that everyday language does mix them, leads us to muddles and pseudoproblems when we embark on discussions of those problems which have traditionally been regarded as the subject-matter of philosophy. When, for example, the word 'house' is used as object in the sentence 'John perceives a house' it belongs to person-language. When it is subject of the sentence 'This house is tall' it belongs to impersonal language. The two languages describe two quite distinct universes of discourse. To mix the two languages, to regard the nouns as standing for entities existing side by side in one and the same world and standing in some objective relation, such as cause and effect, to each other, is absurd. To ask how the "real" house is objectively related to John's house-percept is to raise a pseudo-problem. It is about as rational as trying to locate on a map of England the scene of Alice's adventures through the looking-glass.

We can elucidate the issue before us by considering the case of a motorist seeing a road sign—say a green light—and acting accordingly. We can describe this, legitimately, in either of two ways. First, we can talk in impersonal language, i.e. use fictions and say that a vast collection of atoms, composing the sign, each consisting of electrons and a nucleus, are in such a state that they send forth energy-waves of a certain length and frequency. These come into contact with the eye of a physical organism, and cause a disturbance in the atoms composing the optic nerve. This disturbance, which is, of course, different if the frequency is X from what it is if the frequency is Y, travels up to the brain and initiates a reaction of the whole organism which is different in the X case from what it is in the Y case. The whole of this description—stimulus and reaction—is in terms of the motion of bodily particles in a three-dimensional physical medium. There is no reference to any conscious experience or decision; there are no psychological concepts. Secondly, we can describe this same event in person-language. The person sees the green percept and thinks "Good! I can go ahead". He then initiates changes in his perceived-world, which may be accompanied by changes in other people's perceived-worlds. There is no reference to "the" world.

Now both these ways of describing the event are, in separation, legitimate. But to mix the languages and talk of a brain disturbance causing a sensation of green in the motorist's "mind" is nonsense. We can either talk about the Universe in impersonal sentences, in terms of particles of matter in motion, or else talk about it as a community of selves, each with his private perceived-world, *but we must not talk about it in both these ways in the same context,* for the functions of the two languages, and their relation to reality, are quite different. To illustrate the kind of confusion to which the mixing of these languages leads, let us return to our motorist.

When we mix our languages, the whole process is conceived as a series of events in time, each of which is the effect of what precedes and the cause of what follows, the earliest and latest being "physical" and the middle ones being "mental". The fact that the time series is short does not affect the argument; the point is that there is conceived to be a time-series of events, and that the motions of the higher centres of the brain are regarded as occurring after, and as a result of, the events in the lamp and in the ether. These brain-events are conceived to *cause* the seeing of the green sense-datum, and this mental event in its turn causes a physical reaction. Now if I were to say that it seems very strange that the mere motions of brain-particles should cause people to see colours, the reader would be entitled to answer: "Out of your own mouth I confute you. For you have already insisted that no one causal sequence is more mysterious than another. Effects do not have to *resemble* their causes; they merely follow them regularly. There is nothing more mysterious in the following of brain-motions by visual sensations than in the following of the pressing of a switch by the glowing of a lamp."

But far from helping the defender of the mixed or matter-mind language, this answer only serves to reveal the hopeless difficulties in which he has landed himself. For if my and your consciousnesses of our perceived-worlds are the effects of causes, then, since effects do not have to resemble their causes, what grounds have we for claiming to know *anything at all* about objective entities which cause, or an Entity which causes, our perceivings? But to claim to know that a material world of electrons and waves and nervous systems causes what we perceive is to claim to know quite a lot about it. The self-contradiction is complete.

This discussion of the alleged causal connection between brain-motions and the seeing of a light is not intended, *by itself*, to demonstrate that there cannot be a world-in-itself. I have already given other and sound reasons for rejecting that concept. But it does expose the absurdity of the notion of a causal inter-action between a "physical" and a "mental" world, and in particular the absurdity of the notion of a causal inter-action between brain and mind. This is not, of course, to say that the language of physics and physiology is false. It can be true, in the sense of the word 'true' which we have seen to be appropriate to impersonal language. But we must not regard the language of physics and physiology as describing *causes* of conscious experience. The language of physics and physiology is parallel or alternative to language about conscious experience.

A good example of the fallacy of regarding personal language and impersonal language as both applicable to the same universe of discourse is Descartes's attempt to discover the point at which the mind makes contact with the brain. His problem was a pseudo-problem. There is no sense in asking where consciousness intervenes in the physical-physiological process, because talk about consciousness is not appropriate to the impersonal-language universe of discourse. If we are going to talk about conscious processes we should use language in which the word 'thing' means perceived-object or percept in someone's field of consciousness. We must *either* use the matter-motion language or the community-of-souls language, but we must not use them in the same context and think that they refer to one and the same "world". We can, if we like, think of the matter-motion language as parallel, *as a whole*, to the personal language. But this is not "psycho-physical parallelism" in the sense in which the term was formerly used in text-books of psychology. The idea behind that term was that there were two processes, psychical and physical, which ran parallel. But I am not contending that there are two separate objective processes. There is only one real process, and person-language is the only way for us to describe it when we are seeking philosophical accuracy. Persons, i.e. conscious wholes each with his own perceptual world, really do exist. But impersonal language about a common material world of inorganic and organic bodies, is language about *symbols* or *signs* of conscious existence. In using impersonal language of this sort we are, in fact, using a *double* symbolism. First there are the word-symbols—words like 'chair' and 'bodily organism'; second there are the fictions or "as if" pictures which these words call up—our mental pictures of a three-dimensional world of inorganic bodies and material organisms existing in a common time and space. But these pictures themselves are only symbolism—of very great practical utility, and indeed indispensable for the business of living our lives, but symbolism nevertheless. The pictures of bodily organisms symbolize conscious beings; the symbol of "The material universe" symbolizes the Objective Mind of God.

8

THE COSMOLOGIST'S FALLACY

We are now in a position to see that one's expertness in that abstruse sphere where advanced physics and astronomy meet—the sciences of cosmology and cosmogony—does not confer on one any special authority to pronounce on human destiny. These sciences are conducted in impersonal language, in the sense in which I have used this term, and they share the fictional or "as if" character of all physical science. The "truth" of the cosmologist's findings is not a matter of simple correspondence with objective fact. To say that an impersonal scientific sentence is true is merely to say that the future experiences which it leads us to expect, or which it leads us to infer that we should have had at some past time, will occur or would have occurred, as the case may be. It is clear, then, that when the physicist tells us that millions of years ago the universe, or some part of it, consisted of gaseous matter or of a nothingness which somehow had the capacity of turning itself into bits of energy, or when the geologist tells us that a certain process took place millions of years before there was any consciousness to experience it, they are saying something of a very curious nature, something which, although in a sense true, is true only in a very peculiar sense, something which

96

cannot be taken at its face value but which needs philosophical analysis. Let me give an example of what I have in mind.

Suppose the head of a factory were to explain to a visitor a system whereby the staff were changed round from job to job so as to avoid boredom, and suppose he produced a chart enabling one to calculate which workman, on any past or future date, had been or would be at a given machine. Now the visitor might borrow the chart and, if he were that kind of person, calculate what machine William Jones would have been operating on the day on which Henry VIII came to the throne, or what machine he will be using on April 1st in the year A.D., 30,000 if he lives as long. All this would be quite legitimate reasoning; it really would follow logically from the chart, and therefore be true.

But the calculation would, of course, be futile, for neither William Jones nor the factory existed when Henry VIII came to the throne and they will presumably not exist in the year A.D. 30,000 The futility of the proceeding lies in the fact that a calculating device useful over a short range of time has been used as though it applied to a long period, and the results therefore have no possible bearing on any human problem. Now since the impersonal language used by scientists cannot be claimed to represent reality in any simple and direct way— its function being merely to provide practical guidance for dealing with our sense experience—the use of it to "describe" the state of affairs "vast ages before the existence of human beings" (to use the mixed language which I have criticized) is quite valueless as an objective picture of reality, and quite incapable, therefore, of affording data for speculation about man's importance and destiny, although it is a quite legitimate, and indeed fascinating, intellectual exercise. The cosmologist is, indeed, treating physics as our factory visitor

G   97

treated the chart. His language about the state of the solar system "vast ages ago" is merely an indication of what beings with faculties like ours would have experienced at a time when, by hypothesis, no such beings existed. Impersonal language must be translated into personal language before it can have a simple correspondence with reality, and if, therefore the cosmologist is to tell us anything important the Person whose experience he needs to describe is God. Since God's experience presumably transcends our finite time and space awareness, this task is presumably beyond the cosmologist, as such.

Anyone who has followed the argument so far will see that talk about consciousness "emerging" out of "matter" in the course of an objective time-process is nonsense, if for no other reason than that it exhibits human consciousness as a product of one of its own fictions. It is amazing that a writer of the standing of Lord Russell should make such a statement as the following: "That man is the product of causes which had no prevision of the end they were achieving; that his origin, his growth, his hopes and fears, his loves and beliefs, are but the outcome of accidental collocations of atoms . . . if not quite beyond dispute, is yet . . . nearly certain. . . ."[1] The only certainty about this statement is that it is nonsense.

It is easy, now, for us to see the absurdity of talk about the "littleness" of man compared with the vastness of the Universe. To predicate size and spatial relations of the whole signified by the sentence 'He cognizes spatial relations' is but another instance of the error of mixing personal with impersonal language. Again, to belittle man because of the brevity of his earthly life as compared with the vast ages of geological or astronomical time is absurd, for, as we have seen, we have no right to tear the abstract concept of tem-

[1] Quoted by Professor H. J. Paton in his Gifford lectures—*The Modern Predicament*, page 108.

poral succession from that essential relation to the ego which gives us a concrete existent. We cannot significantly speak of time-in-itself. Time is always time-for-someone; the "real value" of man is his value for God.

A not uncommon but fallacious merging of the personal and the impersonal language-standpoints occurs when, in viewing a sunset, men say that the reality is the electrons and wave-motions and that the beauty is merely a subjective effect in our minds. When we are at the standpoint of a sound philosophy—the standpoint of pure personal language—we see that the situation is the very reverse of this. The beauty is as immediately "given" as is the red and gold; the reality is that persons exist and are impressed by the beauty; language about wave-motions is fictional. Our emotional life provides objective data for our philosophizing far more relevant than those fictional concepts which serve us in our practical commerce with our sensory experience.

We have, in short, to face the fact that if we are to speculate about man's value and destiny—and to refuse to do so is to refuse to obey instincts which, more than any other human characteristics, differentiate us from the animals—we must do so in personal language. Impersonal language affords no guide when we exercise our fundamental human right to speculate about God, moral responsibility and immortality. The more abstract a science, the less speculative light it sheds. Mathematics and pure logic, mechanics and physics, astronomy and cosmology are almost irrelevant—although even they can impress us with the systematic unity of the Universe. Speculation must be based on a study of the consciousness of man. We are much nearer the heart of reality when we study human history. But even here we must differentiate. The economic aspects of history, for example, offer very little for constructive philosophy. The most valuable

CHRISTIAN RATIONALISM AND PHILOSOPHICAL ANALYSIS

data for philosophy are offered by the history of man's philosophic thought and religious experience. After all, where is one more likely to find a revelation *from* God than in the study of men's search *for* God?

100

9

THE ANALYSIS OF STATEMENTS
ABOUT GOD

W e have made a clear-cut division between personal and impersonal language—between sentences the grammatical subjects of which indicate finite conscious beings and sentences the grammatical subjects of which are material-object or scientific-object nouns. We claimed that the former sentences had a simple and direct relation to the objective situation which cannot be claimed for the latter. Personal nouns, we saw, can be reified; there really are Williams and Johns. But impersonal nouns cannot. Their objective reference is merged in that of the whole sentence which contains them, and the objective reference of this whole sentence is by no means simple and direct.

I now wish to argue that sentences the grammatical subjects of which are the word 'God' occupy as it were a position intermediate between these two extremes. I shall aim at showing that although these sentences cannot be claimed to have, in their entirety, that simple and direct relation to reality which true sentences about the experiences of finite beings have, nevertheless they have by no means the wholly fictional character of impersonal language. As regards their grammatical *subject*, the word 'God', they are much nearer to personal language and share its simple and direct relation to reality. In other words, we can validly reify the word 'God'. But as regards their *predicates*, they must, at any rate to some extent, be interpreted as elliptical references to our own experience.

With regard to our right to reify the word 'God', we have already seen[1] sound reason for believing in an Objective Mind. When we rejected the concept of a material world-in-itself we had to offer an alternative explanation of the difference between the public nature of perception and the private nature of imagination. We saw that the concept of an Objective or Standard Awareness gave us what we needed. It gave us an objectively real world, defined as the World-for-the-Standard-Observer, and it avoided the absurdity of a material world-in-itself which was a hypostatized abstraction. We thus arrived at the concept of God *incidentally*, and this, as we saw, showed how inevitable, how vitally related to our everyday perceptual experience, the thought of God became. We cannot, of course, know what *sort* of being objects have for God; we cannot see them as He sees them when no finite being sees them. We cannot even assume that God's experience is conditioned by those forms of time and space which condition ours. But we can be sure that corresponding to what is "real" to us, in the sense of perceived by us, there is something in His awareness, and that this something guarantees the objectivity of our percepts as distinct from our private imaginings. (Not, of course, that even our private imaginings need be thought of as *unknown* to Him.)

So much for the grammatical subject of the sentences about God. But as regards the predicates, it is quite obvious that many statements about God's "nature" and "activities" are anthropomorphic; they are pictures adapted to the limitations

[1] In Chapter 3.

102

of *our* mental powers, and we must interpret them by refering to certain of *our* experiences which give them an "as if" or analogical truth. (We can even use the term 'fictional', for we have carefully ruled out any suggestion that this term connotes falsity.)

To summarize, then, so far. If I say "William is angry" I claim that both subject and predicate of this sentence correspond to reality in a simple and direct way. If I say "Iron is heavy" or "Silence is golden" I cannot claim that either subject or predicate has this simple relation to reality. If I say "God is good" or "God is angry" I claim that while the subject can validly be reified, the predicate must be interpreted analogically and justified by reference to human experience.

I must now deal with an objection. The reader may point out that so far I have only shown that it is more reasonable to refer to the ultimate ground of existence as "He" rather than "It". But when we have established our right to use a personal pronoun we still, he may say, have to show that it must be a singular personal pronoun and not a plural one.

The answer is simple. As we saw in Chapter 1, the speculative or metaphysical instinct the possession of which distinguishes us from the beasts of the field is essentially an instinct to seek *unity*. The scientist, for example, seeks a coherent, i.e. a unified, view of the aspect of reality which he studies. He is never content to reduce his scientific descriptions to separate laws; he always seeks to show these laws as mutually involved —as implying one another or as both implied by a more ultimate law. Now the onus of proof lies on him who *denies* connection between the "structure" of our minds and the structure of reality—between our intellectual instincts and the data which our intellects study, for thought and reality are not separate entities separated by a gulf; subject and object are abstractions from a concrete whole. We have, therefore,

103

every right to regard our intellectual "demand" for unity as far more than a demand—as being an insight. We do not, in fact, merely *demand* unity; we know that it is there, and our task is merely to try to see how the essential unity of the universe is related to its plurality. This is abundant justification for saying 'He' rather than 'They'.

But there is another way in which I find Theism far more intellectually satisfying than any other way of conceiving the ultimate nature of reality. I am not claiming that what follows is a logically necessary or tautological proof; indeed, as we have seen, *none* of our beliefs about the real world can be given such proof—not even one's belief that people other than oneself exist. But it is a line of thought which always produces in me an intense conviction that the theist must be right.

The most fundamental question we can raise about the universe is "Why should there be anything at all?" Whether we postulate as our starting-point a system of material particles or bundles of energy or an aggregate of sensa and sensibilia or, finally, God, we still find ourselves asking how they, or how God, "got there in the first place". *This* question is unanswerable by finite beings; we are still left with our question "Why should there be anything at all?" But since the universe *does* exist, there must obviously *be* an answer. If our intellects were capable of functioning adequately on the point we should see the answer—which might mean that we should see why the question is absurd. Now if we have postulated any of these types of entity other than God as our "basic" or "ultimate" reality—that which "really" exists—we are up against a difficulty which does not arise for the theist. For the alleged particles, etc., have produced beings who are capable of asking, and who find themselves impelled to ask, a question to which there must *be* an answer, but it is an answer which neither the universe itself nor any conscious being in it knows. I am not, of course, suggesting that there is any strict logical contradiction in such a state of affairs, but I do, as a rational being, feel it so unsatisfactory as to be quite incredible. The question "Why should there be anything?" is quite legitimate, for the universe produces beings who ask it inevitably. The answer is "there"—is somehow "in" the universe—for the universe, by existing, proves that the question is answerable, if only in the sense of exposing the absurdity of the question. And yet there is nowhere in the universe an intellect capable of knowing the answer. I find this perfectly fantastic. The universe which raises the question in my own mind must know the answer. This conviction certainly reinforces the arguments for Theism which I have outlined. Whatever more there may be in reality, there must at least be an awareness of the absurdity of the suggestion that there might have been no reality. Reality must include *complete* self-awareness, including comprehension of its own necessity. There is much in Hegel which I find obscure, but I cannot doubt that he and Aristotle were right in seeing Reality as complete self-realization transcending all implicit or potential awareness—as actual awareness baffled by no brute facts.

10

HUMAN FREEDOM AND DIVINE OMNISCIENCE

Another example of a pseudo-problem arising from the confusion of language standpoints is the alleged problem of the "freedom of the will". At the level of impersonal language we use the fictional or "as if" concept of a three-dimensional world-in-itself occurring in a time order identical for all observers and stretching indefinitely into the past and the future. We have found it useful, in such sciences as mechanics, to suppose that all particles of matter are regulated by mathematical laws and that, therefore, if there were a mind in the universe sufficiently competent to take note of the positions and momenta of all particles at any moment of this alleged common time, he would be able to predict with absolute accuracy the position and momentum of any particle at any future moment. Now this is only a supposition; there is no way of proving that it applies to the particles forming the cells of living organisms. Many scientists deny, even, that it is applicable in atomic physics; they point out that there is no evidence that electrons behave in accordance with this theory. All this goes to show with what caution, and with what reservations, scientists ought to speak of the *truth* of determinism, *even from the standpoint of impersonal language*. But the height of absurdity is reached when this dubious concept of determinism is dragged, so to speak, into the personal language scene, and made to do duty there even at the cost of denying the immediate acquaintance of a person with his freedom of choice.

If it were true that my every bodily activity was completely determined by this kind of mechanical causation, then the fact that some intelligence in the Universe had calculated some action of mine in advance and told me what I was going to do could not prevent my doing it. For on this theory I merely look on my bodily activities as a spectator, since they all could have been predicted before my birth. Now this theory is clearly false, for if the intelligence in question were to tell me that in ten seconds I should still be sitting down I should promptly stand up. You cannot escape the contradiction by saying that this only proves that I had really been predestinated to stand up, for on the determinist theory we are justified in postulating that an infallible mathematical intelligence had done the sum correctly, and that I had, therefore, really been predestinated to sit down. Nor can you challenge my right to select an instance where there was no *external* veto on my action, for the determinist theory claims to cover such cases.

The only way by which the determinist can escape the difficulty is by adding a stipulation about his deterministic universe, namely that its causal laws must be of such a nature that either no intelligence capable of making the calculation can be produced, or else an intelligence capable of making the calculation must be unable to communicate his findings to the person whose actions have been calculated. But a theory loses its impressiveness when you have to start adding detailed *ad hoc* conditions to make it work. Almost any theory can be saved if it is made clumsy enough.

107

These objections to determinism as a theory of human conduct are, of course, overwhelming, but they are only incidental to my main thesis. My real objection is that there is not the slightest reason for holding that personal concepts are less ultimate than or must be reduced to, the impersonal concepts of mechanics or physics. We have seen that such a theory would be the reverse of the truth. The concepts of personal language have a simple and direct reference to the objective situation which the fictional concepts of physics and mechanics lack.

Once we have grasped this vital truth, we shall escape the temptation to jump from the frying-pan of determinism into the fire of an indeterminism which would depict the universe as a chaos in which blind chance reigns. Determinism and indeterminism are both essentially concepts of impersonal language.

Let me approach the consideration of the question of indeterminism in general by considering the concept of indeterminacy as used in modern atomic physics.

The point I am immediately concerned to make is that language about indeterminacy must be interpreted subjectively and not objectively, and that this is very relevant to my insistence that we must not reify the nouns used in physics.

What exactly is meant when we say that a revolving particle spends on the average x times as much time on one orbit as on another but that so long as this condition is fulfilled it is free to jump from one orbit to another at any instant—the times of the individual jumps being undetermined? Can we feel any confidence that we are talking sense if we say that a particle possesses, objectively or "in itself", a negative property—the property of *not* being compelled to jump when in fact it does jump? The fact that on the average it spends x times longer on one orbit than on the other proves that there is system in the business; it is not pure chaos. Is it not highly probable that the statement that the particle is free, or not compelled, to jump when it does jump derives a spurious appearance of significance from the analogy of freely choosing human beings? It makes sense to say that Jones has to spend ten times longer in London than in Paris but within these limits is free to go to Paris and return when he likes. But a dead particle cannot choose to jump the orbits "when it likes".

In fact, talk about indeterminacy in objective terms is suspiciously like a fairy tale. We had better confine ourselves to facts, and avoid unnecessary speculation. It is *our knowledge* that is indeterminate; it is *we* who cannot "determine" —in the sense of "know precisely"—what makes the particle jump when it does. And this affords a yet further indication that we are on the right lines when we say that the notion of a particle "in itself"—in this case an electron—is fictional or "as if". For even if we insist that the electron is an entity-in-itself, we have to endow it with "as if" *properties*; we have to say "It is *as though* it knew it had to spend x times longer on one orbit than on another, but was able to choose to jump whenever it took a fit into its head". Surely it is safer to go the whole hog, and endow it not merely with fictional properties but with fictional existence. In this case we say "The phenomena observed in our laboratories are *what they would be if* an electron existed and if it felt compelled to spend x times as long here as there but if it could choose, within these limits, the times of its jumps". In support of this, there is the fact that we find it better, or even necessary, sometimes to drop the electron notion altogether and talk of waves.

So much for the physical concept of indeterminacy. I have written enough to show that it is quite irrelevant to the question of human freedom of choice. Physical indeterminism is essentially an impersonal language concept and, as we have seen, impersonal language envisages a universe of discourse quite different from that of personal language. We must not mix the language or the entities. Even if we were able to regard impersonal language about indeterminacy as objective—even if, that is, we could get round the difficulty about intrinsic negativity—our concept would throw no light on the freedom of human choice. For to say that something is, objectively, *not* determined, is very far from saying that it has freedom of choice, that it can *act*, and act *spontaneously*. The "freedom" of a dead particle would be something very different from the conscious freedom of choice of a living being. And if, on the other hand, we frankly admit that the language of mechanics and physics is fictional, and that language about indeterminism is language about our subjective inability to "determine" in the sense of "know", our physical concept is equally irrelevant to the question of human freedom of choice. To say that we do not know why something happens is very far from saying that it happens "for no reason at all"—from saying, that is, that reality is a realm of chaos and blind chance.

In discussing human freedom of choice, then, we must free ourselves from the influence of the concepts of physics and mechanics. We must come to the examination of our conscious experience with no bias. We must just sit down humbly before the facts. The discussion must be conducted entirely in the terms of personal language. We shall not talk of particles and forces but of conscious selves, with their experiences of *feeling* compelled or *feeling* free. We have emancipated ourselves from the subconscious feeling that human freedom must somehow be explained away.

First, let us analyse statements in personal language about freedom of choice. We shall then have to face the problem of reconciling the concept of positive, personal freedom with

110

that conception of reality as systematic which is inherent in our rationality.

To get to the heart of the question of human freewill, we have to examine the theory that when people think they are freely choosing between two alternative courses of action they are really being *compelled* to take the one which they do take. We have seen that all appeals to the concepts of mechanics or physics are irrelevant, and we therefore have to ask whether there is anything *in the experience itself* to justify the statement that one is compelled. The answer is "No". One has a perfectly clear consciousness of being free to choose and there is nothing in the experience itself to suggest doubts on the subject. If there is no physical compulsion to choose course A rather than course B—if, that is, one is able to take either course if one wishes to do so—then one is free to choose, and there is nothing more to be said. I am not, of course, claiming that at the personal language thought-level we can dismiss as illusion the notion that the conduct of living creatures is influenced by hereditary and environmental factors. There are obviously vast differences between the psychological structures, so to speak, with which people begin their lives, and an infant's moral development is influenced by suggestion and teaching. We can quite legitimately speak of making allowances for people's moral disadvantages. But there is one class of statements which we cannot allow, namely first person singular statements in the present tense in the following form: "I am at this moment being compelled by my inherited character and early training (or by my glands or my neurosis or my inhibitions) to act in a certain way although there is no external or physical compulsion to do so". This statement is nonsense, and derives an appearance of sense only by an illegitimate appeal to a sophisticated metaphysical theory derived from mechanics. We must not obliterate the distinction between "I will" and "I must". If there is external or physical compulsion "I must" is appropriate; if there is none, then one must say "I will". It may be that we can appropriately use the "must", the language of compulsion, when we are talking of the "choices" of conscious beings who are not *self*-conscious—beings who cannot say to themselves "I exist and I am now called upon to make a choice". But when a person *is* self-conscious, when he is capable of becoming aware of the fact that he has been subject to such and such influences —then his awareness of this fact renders him "free to choose", in the sense that it is *he* who is choosing. Indeed, to say "I am free to choose", or "It is I who am choosing", or "I am responsible for my choice" is to say the same thing in different ways. When I drag up from my unconscious—or otherwise become aware of—a factor which has hitherto been a compulsion, it ceases to be a compulsion. The appropriate word is 'temptation'.

I am not here discussing the questions of blame or punishment or the treatment of offenders. I am saying nothing intended to lessen sympathy with people who have chosen wrong courses. I am merely concerned with the importance of making a distinction of language when there is a clear distinction of cases. When there is no external compulsion we must not use the same terms as when there is external compulsion. We must distinguish between "I will" and "I must". There is no internal compelling force, in the case of a self-conscious being, other than the person himself.

It is important to see that although this defence of language about freedom and moral responsibility resembles in one respect the purely verbal "solution" offered by certain philosophical analysts, it is most certainly *not* a purely verbal solution. The analysts in question point out, quite rightly, that the accepted use of the English language is such that a person is, by definition, "free" to do something when there is no physical obstacle. I am not free to jump over a house but I am free, if in the middle of a field and not paralysed, to walk to the right or to the left. This is true but trivial. But I am not defending the phrase 'I can freely choose' on the mere ground that it is good English. I am insisting that it is an "ultimate" account of an objective situation—in the sense that it cannot, without loss of meaning and truth-value, be translated into the language of compulsion borrowed from physics or mechanics.

This experience of freely choosing is most emphatically *not* an experience of standing aside and watching happenings which we must describe as caused by forces "outside" us or as "due to the operations of blind chance". The experience is of events which are controlled or determined by ourselves. If the action were not controlled by myself I should not admit responsibility for it, but I do most clearly experience it as *my* act; *I* am responsible for it. There is not the slightest reason for trying to explain this experience away, unless we are moved by analogies from alleged physical processes which I have shown to be totally irrelevant. The action is neither determined in the mechanical sense nor undetermined. It is self-determined.

In short, the real universe, as described in personal language, is the field neither of blind chance nor of an equally blind determinism *a tergo* by *earlier* events. It is a realm the systematic connections of which must be studied in the light of such concepts as 'choice', 'purpose', 'end in view'. We have already touched on the concept of the God in whom we live and move and have our being—we have shown how inevitably this concept arises—but we yet have to enquire what can be said, if anything, from the standpoint of philosophy about the relation between the finite beings and God. But it will be relevant here to make the point that the concept of purpose does throw a little more light on the problem—a problem certainly not completely soluble by the human mind—of reconciling the existence and freedom of finite beings with that systematic unity of reality which as rational beings we demand.

In considering this, we must bear in mind that a means to an end need not be *merely* a means to an end. A voyage to America may be a means to some end which can be achieved only by the voyage, but it may also be enjoyed for its own sake; it may in that sense be an end in itself. Again, a person may be pursuing, and indeed achieving, some end which for him is an end in itself, and yet some other person may be using him as a means to *his* ends. We can quite reasonably think of the unity of the Universe as expressing a "Divine Purpose" which is worked out by means of the perfectly free choices of beings who are pursuing, and indeed often achieving, their own ends. This, indeed, is probably the nearest that we human beings can get to solving the problem before us. As we shall see more clearly later, this is only an anthropomorphic or analogical solution, but, as we shall also see, this is no reason for being dissatisfied with it. Our thinking is in the nature of things incurably anthropomorphic, and all that we are required to do as rational beings is to see that it is *critically* so.

But it will be appropriate here to deal with the question why, when two persons, A and B, are confronted with similar situations, do they make different choices? Jones and Brown, we will say, are in exactly similar positions with regard to their financial commitments and, so far as we can see, in their other circumstances. They are of similar *types*; their upbringing and heredity, so far as we can judge, are similar, and yet one succumbs to the temptation to forge a cheque, while the other resists it. We had already excluded the answer that there must be some difference in earlier factors or events which "determines" the decision, in the sense in which that word is used in mechanics. Each person was *free* to *choose*. Why did one's choice differ from the other's?

We must approach the answer to this question by examining the meaning of the question itself. What *sort* of answer can we expect to receive, given that our question relates to the universe of discourse of personal language and not to the fictional realm of impersonal language? We are not asking what earlier factors inevitably "caused" the choice in the sense of "made it inevitable". What then *are* we asking?

Are we to say "The question is meaningless. The very fact that the choice is *free* means that we cannot ask why it was made"? Certainly not. We are not confronted with a choice between on the one hand, mechanically caused "choices" and on the other hand utter chaos and irrationality. A choice may not have a "cause", as that word is used in mechanics, but it may have a reason or purpose. Indeed, if the person is sane, is responsible for his actions, his choices must have reasons or purposes. If they are indeterminate in the sense of chaotic, the person is certainly not morally responsible.

So we are still left with our question "Why did A take one course and B the other?" It is a reasonable question, and yet it is not an enquiry into earlier causal factors.

The answer surely lies in our concept of self-determination. The only person who, in the nature of things, can have all the data for answering it, is the person himself. Only Jones can appreciate the full force of the temptation—only *he* is aware of the influence of all the factors which are operating when he makes the choice. This is not, of course, to say that even *he* can adequately *analyse* them, is *explicitly* aware of them all, and find words with which to convey them to others. But the answer is clear. Only Jones, and God, can experience all the factors. And only God is *explicitly* aware of them all. The factors are *essentially* personal and private.

I think this answer is final, and indeed satisfactory, so far as the question *as it stands* is concerned. But in asking it we often have at the back of our minds a further question or perhaps a series of questions, concerned with praise and blame, reward and punishment. It arises, I think, in this way. We have seen that when we raise the question, why Jones made the moral choice which he did make, we must not say that his action was caused by the blind causality of earlier events and conditions, nor must we say that his action was a matter of mere chance. Jones made the choice he did make because he was at that moment the kind of person he was. *He* determined the action. Now it is easy to explain our praise or blame as the expression of our pleasure or displeasure, our wish to encourage or discourage that kind of choice by members of human society. But such praise or blame refers to the person's actions. Do we, or ought we to, or does God, praise or blame him for being the kind of person he is? Admittedly he must accept responsibility for his "voluntary" actions in the sense that he must own them as *his*; he cannot say, at the moment of his choosing, that he is being compelled by anything but himself. But he did not create himself, he did not choose to *be* that kind of conscious being. Is there, therefore, any question of blaming or punishing him for being what he is?

Up to a point, we can clearly answer "Yes!"—to the point, that is, of saying that his character has been in some measure influenced by earlier voluntary decisions, and that he cannot therefore altogether disclaim responsibility for being the kind of person he is. But in the previous sentence we have had to say "in some measure" and "altogether". We cannot say that a person is *entirely* responsible for being the kind of person he is. He woke up, as it were, and found himself alive with a certain psychological "structure", a certain "temperament".

Now are we prepared to say that whatever the original "structure" with which a person begins life he is free to reach the moral and spiritual standard which any other person has attained? I cannot see that we have sufficient evidence to make this assertion. That rational self-conscious beings are free to rise or fall in the moral scale is certain, and they must accept responsibility for such rise or fall. But heredity and environment would appear to be limiting factors.

These considerations would appear to set a problem for those of us who affirm that one's future destiny—one's "salvation"—one's attaining or failing to attain "eternal life"—depend on one's moral decisions in this earthly life. But the problem becomes acute, it seems to me, only in the case of a legalistic religion which would make salvation dependent on the attainment of a certain moral standard. I cannot help feeling that it was the subconscious or even unconscious influence of this last consideration which led Christian theologians to conceive of salvation as depending on faith rather than on "works". And I think they are plainly right. It seems perfectly rational to maintain that any rational self-conscious person can be held responsible for accepting or rejecting an offer of Divine forgiveness and a *gift* of eternal life. He must, that is, admit that it is his decision; his destiny is not being *forced* on him.

I think we can bring the discussion of this point to a head by considering a simple instance. Suppose a person reasons as follows: "I am going to do something wrong. There are no external factors forcing me to do it, and I agree that it would be quite inappropriate for me to say that my heredity or my past training or lack of it are *forcing* me to do it. It is my *free*

117

choice. But nevertheless I am not to be blamed and ought not to be punished because I did not make myself and if I were other than I am I might not be making this particular free choice." Clearly the objection must be disallowed. He deserves punishment not for being what he is but because, being what he is—a morally free person—he freely chooses the wrong.

I do not see any moral problem in the fact that an infinite variety of finite beings exists with vast differences in their capacities for pleasure and pain, happiness and unhappiness, that of these finite beings many (the animals and lower forms of life) must be presumed to be exterminated by the death of their bodies, and that not all those self-conscious, rational beings capable of receiving "eternal life", will in fact do so. I see no moral problem in the fact that a pig cannot appreciate Mozart, or achieve immortality. We do not blame a tiger for being cruel, but if we are as ruthless in shooting him as he is in tearing a lamb to pieces we do not feel we are wronging him. I am not here concerned with the problem of pain, or the problem of the existence of evil. I shall come to those problems shortly. I am merely concerned to insist that there is a limit beyond which it is meaningless to push our questionings as to the "justice" of the destinies appropriate to the various types of finite being. There is in particular, no moral problem in the fact that beings who can conceive of but do not desire a higher life, and beings who are incapable of conceiving that there *can* be a higher life, will not attain it.

An important question remains. How can we reconcile our belief that men are free and morally responsible with our belief in the systematic unity of Reality—the *completeness* of the Divine awareness or Divine omniscience?

To discuss this adequately, we need to consider the notion of "creation"—the relation between the being of God and the being of men. We have rejected the picture of God as a kind of clock-maker and man as a clock—the picture of God having, at a certain point of past time, put the springs of action inside men, and who is therefore able, because of His exact knowledge of the mechanical laws determining men's actions, to calculate in advance exactly what men are going to do. The fact is, if we use the word 'create' at all in speaking of the relation between God's existence and a man's existence, we use it in an absolutely unique sense. There are no exact analogies *within* the world as we experience it. We must here recall the sentence from Dr. Mace's essay which I quoted in Chapter 1.[1] In speaking of the metaphysical models which we must inevitably use, he said: "All these models . . . look absurd. But not one of them is entirely absurd. Each draws attention to something of interest and importance. Absurdity results when some irrelevant features of the model are attributed to whatever is modelled."

The difficulty which we are facing has arisen from our using irrelevant features of the creation-model. The uniqueness of the relation between God's being and man's can be expressed only by using a *number* of models. We are "born" of God; we "proceed" from God; we "emanate" from God. But all these models contain irrelevances. The inadequacy of all of them lies in the fact that they assume a time process— they suggest an action in time. Now from the human side a man's birth *is* an event in time, but if we define the term 'reality' as 'The universe as it is for God', we are bound to say that reality somehow transcends the time series as we know it. I shall, of course, have later to defend this statement. I make it here because it serves to reinforce the point which I have already made that the relation between God's being and ours is absolutely unique.

But precisely because the relation between God and finite

[1] See page 12.

119

beings is of a unique character, we are exempt from the task, for it is clearly an impossible task, of "explaining" the relation. For when we wish to explain, in the ordinary sense of the word, we begin by classifying—by showing resemblances to something more familiar. I begin to explain the colours in the oil-patch on the road by classifying them with the colours of the rainbow, the fountain, and the prism, and I further explain all these by showing that they are merely instances of a constantly recurring phenomenon—the refraction of light. In the final analysis all scientific explanation is a matter of showing how some particular event is an instance of a general law, and when the limit of *generality* has been reached, when there is no further class into which the law can be put, the limit of *explanation* has been reached. If we can speak at all of the "explanation" of a unique law or unique event, it is only in the sense of describing it as accurately as we can—of finding the most appropriate language for it. It is a brute fact, which we just have to accept.

It is absurd, then, to speak of "explaining" the relation between God and man if by "explaining" we mean finding some exact analogy in the realm of created things. All our models contain irrelevances, although none of them is valueless if used critically. In his book *Mystery and Philosophy*,[1] Mr. Michael B. Foster challenges the assumption of certain analytical philosophers that human thinking about reality consists exclusively in the solving of problems and the re-solving of puzzles—the assumption that all our thinking is a matter of answering our questions and is aimed at the *elimination* of mysteries. He maintains, on the contrary, that Plato was right in holding that human thinking at its highest *contemplates* mysteries. He quotes, with approval, Dr. E. L. Mascall's contention that in addition to problems and puzzles

[1] S.C.M. Press, 1957.

there are *mysteries*. We can analyse such mysteries, but we cannot "comprehend" them in the sense of so seeing them that the element of mystery vanishes. Only God, presumably, can thus comprehend them.

In view of the uniqueness of the God-man relation, and of our decision that the whole discussion must be conducted in personal language, we must reject as inappropriate all expressions borrowed from impersonal language. We must not say that God *caused* man's existence in the way that the weight of the snow *caused* the bough of the tree to snap. We must not say that man *emanates* from God as light from a lamp, or *comes* from God as a spring from the earth. And since we must also reject the mixed language of everyday life as philosophically inadequate, we must not say that man was born of God as a child's body is born of its parents, or that God made the world as a carpenter makes a chair. We need not reject as *absurd* the question "Why does man exist?". The fact that we have still such a deep-rooted desire to ask it, even when we have pushed our criticism of our reasoning powers to its limits, is its sufficient justification. But the only answer we can give is that we exist because God exists.

But there is one other fact about the unique relation between men and God which becomes apparent on analysis. Throughout this book I have considered the being of a man from the "inside", so to speak. I have defined a man as the man experiences himself—as a succession of percepts, emotions and volitions held in unity by their constituting one memory-chain or by their relation to one and the same ego. Now if we assert that two lives, viewed in this way, are exactly similar over their life-times, then we are saying something that can be characterized as self-contradictory—or at any rate as meaningless, in the sense that in the nature of things there can be no evidence to support it. If two chains of experience are exactly similar, then they are not two but one. Consider, for example, what would be involved in the exact duplication of Oliver Cromwell. The second Cromwell would, by hypothesis, stand in the same spatial and temporal relations to the rest of the world and of history as did the first. If you are going to insist on the duplication, you will have to duplicate General Fairfax and Charles I and—in fact—the whole Universe. And even then the assertion would be quite arbitrary; no evidence could be produced. You might as well assert fifty universes while you are about it. The assertion, as I said, can either be said to be self-contradictory, since you assert two-ness but under conditions which are applicable only to unity, or else as meaningless because neither proof nor disproof can be offered. (If someone challenges you to prove that his cat is not two permanently coincident cats, you are entitled to answer that the burden of the proof of the two-ness is on him, and he will have to admit that no proof can be offered.)

Now the fact that complete similarity as between consciousnesses is identity is of no importance in the case of finite beings, for at no period in any two lives is there exact similarity. At the very least they must be experiencing either different spatial perspectives or differences due to the fact that one's experience is later in time than the other's. But since the Divine experience, although transcending the time form, must be held to be all-comprehensive and therefore to include our time-awareness, we can significantly affirm an exact similarity, *and therefore identity*, between any finite experience and some part of the Divine experience. The similarity or identity relation is not, of course, a symmetrical one; everything in my awareness is included in that of God, but there are vast areas of God's awareness which transcend all human awareness. (I would remind the reader, for it is vital, that in thus asserting identity I am not attempting to "explain" anything; we are analysing a Mystery.)

We are now in a position to return to the question which prompted this consideration of the relation between God and man—namely the problem of reconciling the omniscience of God with man's freedom of choice. In view of our discussion it is by no means clear that there is any contradiction to reconcile. The popular notion that there is a contradiction arises from the crude idea of God as a being whose outlook is entirely conditioned by time as we know time, viewing a past which has vanished out of being and a future which has not yet come into being. If the omniscience of such a Being is to be held to include the future actions of the finite beings whom He "made" and who exist completely "outside" Him, then this must only be because those future actions are inexorably determined by present conditions. But none of these conditions hold on the view of God-man relations which we have outlined. God's awareness somehow transcends time although including it. His omniscience must not be held to be a *fore*-knowledge of something to be done at what for Him is a future moment. And we are not "outside" Him. There is, so to speak, an area of identity between what we are and what He is. We saw (page 115) that although there is no blind chance and that every decision, even a free decision of a rational being, accords with the pattern of the Whole, nevertheless the only finite being who can, in the nature of things, know, or rather realize, that full content of the self which decides the self-determined action *is* that self. But although no other *finite* being can realize this content, God realizes it, in virtue of that area of similarity which is identity between His awareness and that of any finite being. I can, therefore, be completely free in the sense that it is I who decide my action and that no other finite being in the nature of things can

123

realize the factors leading to it. But God realizes them all, and therefore my actions which are still "future" to me are known to Him. But not *fore*known. His awareness transcends time altogether.

We have been forced to this construction by the consideration that complete similarity of conscious content is complete identity, and by the fact that in no other way can we steer between the Scylla of blind mechanical determinism and the Charybdis of a completely undetermined—a completely chaotic and irrational—Universe, in neither of which could there be real moral responsibility or freedom. But it leads to what are at first sight very curious results. And yet, as we shall see in Chapter 12 they harmonize remarkably with a curious conviction born in us by religious experience. This coincidence between beliefs hammered out by close reasoning and beliefs arrived at by religious insight is confirmation that we are on right lines.

We are morally responsible beings, beings possessing what common sense has called "freewill". My voluntary moral decisions are *my* decisions. But because my awareness is fully realized by God, is fully included in God's awareness, my purposes are included in the larger Purpose of God. (To speak of God as having Purpose is, of course, to speak anthropomorphically or analogically.) An action can be both an end in itself and a means to a greater end. My life is for me an end in itself. But nevertheless I am part of a larger Purpose. *The only way in which a finite being can be free is by identity with the freedom of God.* God did not put a "faculty" of freedom inside me as a watchmaker puts a mainspring in a watch. The connection between God and men is not external, not mechanical. It is vital, organic; it is the Divine immanence.

11

CHANCE, CAUSALITY AND NATURAL SELECTION

Let us begin by considering *sequences* of events. By a 'sequence' I mean a pair of events in which we particularly notice the order in which the events occur. We can use the symbol AB to symbolize a sequence, A standing for the first event and B for the second. A might, for instance, stand for the throwing of a die, and B for its landing with the six uppermost. Or A might stand for the falling of rain, B for the growing of grass.

But a sequence which merely occurs once does not interest the philosopher. It is the fact that sequences are *repeated* that sets our problem. For there are obviously two kinds of repeated sequence. For example, if we are throwing a die we may happen to throw a six ten times running, or we may toss a penny and get heads ten times running. These repetitions of sequence we call chance repetitions or coincidences. On the other hand there are sequences which we call causal, or purposed, and their repetition we do not call a coincidence, for we conceive of the same cause or the same purpose as controlling them all. The connection of rain falling and grass growing is a causal one, and therefore it *must* be repeated. Or a person may be deliberately *choosing* to place a penny with head upwards ten times running.

In describing the first kind of sequences as chance ones we do not mean that *no* causal factors are at work. The fact that a particular throwing of a penny gives heads may well be determined absolutely, as orthodox science holds, by the original position of the penny in the hand, the direction and amount of the force imposed on it, and the air resistance. We merely mean that there is no law whereby pennies must *always* fall heads; that is why, if we do get a long run of heads, we call it a chance run. This limitation of the meaning of 'chance' is important. It serves to distinguish between the chance which can be the subject of exact mathematical calculation and a chaotic chance which would be mere caprice. For example, I shall refer later to the extreme improbability that all the molecules of air will be in one half of the room, leaving someone gasping for breath in the other. But this calculation of probabilities is possible only because molecules of air do *not* behave in a capricious manner; in actual fact they tend to move in straight lines with unchanged momentum unless affected by an external force, but the calculation would in principle be possible provided their movements conformed to *any* fixed pattern. But if the movements were capricious—if they conformed to *no* pattern, they might all suddenly crowd up into one corner of the room and stay there, *for no reason at all*, and no predictions, therefore, as to future situations could be trusted. Similarly, it is only because human beings are not entirely capricious in their behaviour—because, as we say, "human nature does not change"—that we are able in the light of past experience to forecast with considerable accuracy the percentage of railway travellers who will leave their umbrellas in trains. But why may we expect *a priori*, and why do we verify *a posteriori*, that other things being equal an equal percentage of English travellers will forget their umbrellas over two periods? Surely the answer is that there is no reason why the two percentages should differ. We can generalize this into the law that if there is nothing to *make* differences there will *be* no differences. In short, the mathematical calculation of probabilities is possible only because the Principle of Sufficient Reason appears to be objectively true.

With this important reservation as to the meaning of 'chance', we can return to our quite valid distinction between sequences like the tossing of pennies and sequences like the switching on of lights. In practice we have little difficulty in deciding whether the regularity of a sequence is a chance one, in the sense explained, or is a causal or a purposed one. If anyone chose to argue that *all* sequences are due to chance— that there is *no* objective causality or purpose—we should find it impossible to produce a logically necessary proof that any particular sequence was causal or purposed. But there is, of course, an unlimited number of silly statements which it is quite impossible to disprove by tautological reasoning. In rejecting them we are entitled to say that there is not the slightest reason for believing them and that the burden of proof is on him who asserts them, not on us who deny them. The statement that there is no objective causality or that there are no reasons for regularities of sequence, is clearly a statement which we can reject thus.

The simple truth, then, is that if a sequence is regular enough, whether it occurs in nature or is contrived in a laboratory, we can reasonably (i.e. in accordance with the canons of inductive logic) ascribe it to an objective law. In such a case we do not merely say that A is always followed by B, we say that A *causes* B—that A *must* be followed by B. If you jump off a hundred-foot tower you *must* come to harm. If you send a spark through a mixture of oxygen and hydrogen it *must* explode. There are, of course, certain refinements

127

to be mentioned—the sort familiar to students of inductive logic. For example, we do not say that night causes day; but we do say that the appearance of the sun above the horizon causes objects to be visible. The broad fact is that there are real causal sequences as distinct from merely chance runs.

It is necessary to labour this obvious point because some people have the curious idea that Hume showed belief in objective causality to be absurd. All that Hume did was to draw attention to the fact that the only way of discovering *what* causal laws hold in nature is to notice regularities of sequence; we cannot, in the final analysis, see *why* any particular cause should produce any particular effect. We could not, without any prior experience of the AB sequence, say in advance that A *must* produce B. The fundamental or basic laws can only be known *a posteriori*. We do not know *why* Newton's (or Einstein's) law of gravitation holds. But to notice this is to notice something quite irrelevant to the contention that there are objective causal sequences. To say that we cannot know the reason why B must follow A is one thing. To say that there *is* no reason is quite another.

Unless we admit that there must be a reason for those regularities of sequence which we call causal—that there must be something to *make* B follow A—we must admit that all inductive reasoning is fallacious. There is no reason whatever for arguing from the regularity of a sequence in the past to the reasonableness of expecting it to hold in the future unless we proceed via this intermediate postulate "There must be some objective reason or ground or cause for the regularity". The whole of induction depends on admitting that the distinction between chance coincidences of sequence and causal sequences is a distinction *in kind*. Unless there are such things as really *causal* sequences, successful inductions—such as our proving right when we expect the light to come on when the switch is pushed—are merely lucky guesses, and it is unreasonable to expect the run of luck to continue.

In short, any inference from past to future assumes that events conform to some pattern which is either irrelevant to time or which persists over the time period with which the inference is concerned. If I argue that because something has happened nine times out of ten in the past it may be expected to happen nine times out of ten in the future, provided conditions remain unchanged, I am assuming that these unchanged conditions are causal or determining conditions.

The objection has sometimes been made that we have no experience of real links between events—that we experience events as accompanying or succeeding one another but not as influencing one another. But this is not true. We directly experience the form of connection which we call volition. It is a false analysis of the experience of volition to treat it as the *a posteriori* discovery of a mere time-succession of volition and event willed. The experience of deciding to raise an arm and then experiencing the raising is a complex unity; we experience a connected whole and we analyse it into, or abstract from it, the volition and the event as two separate events. We are committing the Humian fallacy—the fallacy which vitiates his whole treatment of cognition—if we imagine that we experience events as separate. Indeed, if we had no experience of connection (in this case the connection of volition) where did we get the *notion* of connection? Our experience is, from the very outset, an experience—however dim, vague or implicit—of a connected unity. Those aspects of it which we fix by prepositions and verbs are as real as those which we fix with nouns.

It may very well be that our notion of real causation—our conviction that if A happens B *must* happen—is a projection of our sense of active volition. This idea fits beautifully our argument that we are justified in thinking of reality in terms of objective Mind or Will.

I have prefaced my consideration of natural selection by these considerations—which some of my readers may think rather obvious—because it is important to notice the background against which certain scientists appear to claim that the species have evolved "by chance". What exactly have we to take for granted before we come to grips with the biological controversy? First, we have to assume the objective time and space framework to which I have referred in the course of this book. I have already explained why this must be regarded as fictional, but for the purpose of this section I will not press this point. If you insist that it is not fictional but that a universe of particles of matter or energy moving in three-dimensional space in objective time exists "in itself", then you are confronted by an inscrutable mystery. The man with enthusiasm for "blind chance" and a passion for getting rid of the notion of purpose will not, of course, admit that *God* created the world, and as he has no alternative explanation he must admit that the existence of the time-and-space framework with its particles or energy-bundles is an inscrutable mystery. Surely he will not claim to have solved the problem by the theory that nothingness turned itself into a highly organized something "by chance"!

It is clear, then, that his "explanation"—even if he can produce it—of the evolution of the species by non-purposive selection of chance variations is going to be an extremely limited affair. He has to swallow a very large camel, and he can use his "chance" strainer to keep out only a small gnat. There is not only creation to be swallowed—but the fact that the movements of the particles and energy-bundles are by no means random ones but are governed by the laws discovered by mechanist, physicist and chemist.

But *will* the strainer keep out even this small insect? Can we rule out purpose in evolution?

Assuming our particles moving in accordance with the scientific laws we have just mentioned, the thesis before us is that without purpose or aim "in" or "behind" the process the dead particles gradually formed themselves into living organisms of a comparatively simple character, and that these, still without there being anywhere any intention, explicit or implicit, to achieve ends, evolved *by chance* into ever more complex forms and finally achieved the various species including the human race. In this process natural selection played an important part, but only, of course, in a negative way. It weeded out the inefficient—the organisms less well adapted to their environment, but it could begin to operate only when a degree of evolution had taken place. It did not *positively* cause eyes and ears and limbs to come into being, it only insured that once organisms with these organs *had* come into being the best specimens tended to survive and produce their kind. Our argument at this point, therefore, is not concerned with natural selection but with the coming into being of that highly complex state of affairs which *had* to exist if natural selection was to have a chance of operating.

The central issue, then, is this. Can we accept the view that, within the time allowed by geologists and physicists, the organisms upon which natural selection has worked could have produced themselves by mechanical or physical or chemical laws—laws in which the future is inexorably determined *by the past alone* and in which what happens at any moment must never, can never, be explained as happening "so as to bring about" a future result?

Now a blindly mechanical system might, of course, produce by pure chance the sort of result which a conscious being could produce by intention. Dust blown by the wind might settle on the ground to make the letters of Shelley's *Ode to a Skylark*. Indeed, I suppose that one could argue that if the world lasted long enough all possible combinations of dust-particle formations would be exhausted and that Shelley's poem and all other poems would be so written. But can we believe that within the time period with which we are concerned the whole ordered, continuous ever-evolving process (which incidentally produced not only Shelley's poem but also Shelley—and Shakespeare and a few others!) could have taken place in this haphazard manner?

What would such a belief involve? To begin with, what would be the mathematical probability that a number of molecules, equal to the number in the human eye, would produce by pure chance in certain circumstances a human eye? We could answer this only by specifying the circumstances in detail, but it would be pointless to do so, for the problem is almost infinitely more complicated than the formation of a single human eye. I begin thus because I want to deal at once with a possible objection. "How do you know", someone may say, "that there are not laws, just as non-purposive or non-teleological, just as 'blind' or '*a tergo*' as are mechanical laws, but nevertheless laws in accordance with which the inorganic *must* turn into the organic, and the organic *must* develop specialized organs like eyes and legs?"

Now our objector is out to dispense with the notion of purpose. He rejects the view that organic bodies develop eyes *in order that* they may see and legs *in order that* they may walk. The existence, then, of a law whereby eyes and legs are produced would itself be merely a matter of chance. So the objection amounts to this—that we need not say that an eye and a leg has evolved by a fluke, for there is (by a fluke) a law whereby an eye and a leg *must* evolve. This is a distinction with very little difference!

There seem, in fact, to be but three broad possibilities:

1. Biology is only complicated chemistry. No teleological language is *required* in biology although (for some curious reason!) teleological language is not merely convenient but almost inevitable (e.g. "the struggle for existence"). It was only "by chance", in the sense explained, that the variations were produced on which natural selection has operated.

2. Evolution can be explained only by postulating that there was, in living organisms, over and above the laws of physics and chemistry, a tendency for ever more and more complex forms to be produced, and for organisms to adapt themselves to their environment by producing the organs required. Eyes were produced *in order that* organisms should see. So far as the organisms themselves are concerned, there was, of course, no conscious purpose in this. We have to postulate an immanent teleology which, as it were, *used* the organisms but of which they were unconscious.

3. The whole of the evolution took place in accordance with (1), by blind mathematical laws. No *innate* tendencies or implicit purposes need be postulated. But it is nonsense to say that the blind laws could have produced the evolution within the time unless they had been specially designed for that purpose. The laws, and the original collocations of the particles, must all have been contrived by a Designer. Evolution is not *innately* purposive; it works quite blindly, but produces results intended by the original external Designer. The evolutionary scheme works like a machine—a mousetrap or an electronic calculator—which is itself quite aimless but which blindly mediates the aims of its inventor.

Now since I regard as fictional the whole conception of particles-in-themselves moving in a time-in-itself, I am relieved of the necessity of regarding any one of these three views as expressing final metaphysical truth. But if we *are* going to discuss reality in these fictional terms, it is clear that the metaphysical construction which I have advocated would favour (2) and reject the blind causality of (1) and (3). But it would supplement the implicit or unconscious teleology of (2) by the conscious teleology of (3). Not, of course, that it would use the term "Designer"—for that suggests a God whose awareness is like ours, an awareness of succession—a God who contrived the machine vast ages ago. But the notion in (2) of *unconscious* purpose is defective. In reality, i.e. for God, all is explicit or actual, and the unconscious teleology of (2) must express something actual in the Divine awareness —something which we predicate analogically as conscious purpose.

In what follows I will try to indicate the reasons, additional to those inherent in my general philosophical position, for my rejection of (1). I am not, of course, required to produce a logically necessary proof that the evolutionary process could not possibly have been due solely to the chance working of purely mechanical or physical or chemical laws. For any chance whatsoever, however fantastically improbable, *might* have come off. But if I read in the popular press that last week a mechanical device for working a typewriter by purely random hits happened to type out *Bleak House* without a mistake, I could not be described as prejudiced if I flatly refused to believe it.

To begin with, let me refer to the point I have already made. If *everything* could be explained by an appeal to blind chance I might feel some temptation to accept the explanation. If, by appealing to chance, we could banish all mystery, could show that our sense of the mystery of existence is illusory—show that there *are* no mysteries, we should be tempted to make the appeal. But the great mysteries remain, even if we profess to believe that the species evolved by natural selection of chance variations. Why anything at all? How did the laws of physics come into being? Since natural selection of so-called chance variations can explain so little, we certainly cannot feel any confidence that the species *must* have evolved by chance. We cannot trust any predilection for chance we may happen to have.

With these considerations in mind, let us look very broadly at the facts. I say "very broadly", for a philosopher, as such, is not qualified to express an authoritative opinion on the detailed argument in such a book as Professor Graham Cannon's *The Evolution of Living Things*.[1] He produces what appears to me to be very strong evidence that the evolution of the species cannot be explained entirely by the natural selection of chance variations, and that Lamarck was right in postulating the operation of special biological laws whereby, when the surroundings of an organism change, a reaction is produced in the organism whereby if new organs are needed they begin to appear, and that proportionately as they are used they develop. (He holds, incidentally, that *this* is Lamarck's most valuable contribution to the subject, not his better-known theory that acquired characteristics can be inherited.) Professor Cannon's view appears to be more or less identical with the second of the three possible views I outlined (he speaks, however, of a Power behind the process). He has made out a very strong case, but as I am not a biologist I cannot enter into details, and can only discuss the question broadly.

I will try to outline my reasons for finding view (1) incredible. In Max Born's book, *The Restless Universe*, he tells us that the number of ways in which 100 molecules could arrange themselves with 50 in the right-hand half of a containing vessel and 50 in the left-hand half is 10,000,000,000,000

[1] Manchester University Press, 1958.

times greater than the number of ways in which they could arrange themselves with 90 in the right and 10 in the left. But there are, of course, vastly more than 100 molecules in a room, and he adds that although it is theoretically possible for all the molecules in a room to get into one half, so that a person in the other half would gasp for breath, the whole history of the human race from the "missing link" to our ultimate posterity would not give sufficient time for it to happen even once.

Now this particular example does not, of course, bear very directly on the problem before us. But when we consider the vast number of molecules in a human eye, it suggests that the odds against these molecules doing not a simple thing like crowding into one half of a container, but arranging themselves into a lens and an optic nerve *by pure chance*, are astronomical. Could it have happened *by chance* in the period between the first appearance of life on the earth and the appearance of the first eye? One might well doubt it, but in any case what actually occurred was something almost infinitely more complicated than this. For the eye was not just momentarily formed, merely to disintegrate again, but it persisted as an eye, over a period of time—by sheer luck! But, of course, the mere possession of an eye would not give an organism an advantage in the struggle for existence unless there were some very complicated accompaniments, such as a mouth, muscles, limbs, and so on, *all in correlation* so that they function as a unity. All this happened to get formed by luck. But even now we have not finished. By pure chance *two* organisms were formed which could enter into sex relations and reproduce an organism of the same kind, and the same fluke was repeated by the second, third, fourth . . . generation. And finally—perhaps the greatest fluke of all—this line of descent occurs not once, not twice, but millions of times, for when we speak of an eye, a vertebrate, a man, we are speaking only of a *specimen*. But there is a whole species.

It might here be objected, however, that we are not multiplying the improbabilities when we point to the fact that there is not one organism but many, not one line of descent, but many. For, it might be said, the conditions which produce one organism in any one place will, wherever they occur, tend to produce similar organisms. The answer is that if you are appealing to chance you are not entitled to argue thus. You must take your appeal to chance seriously. If the production of an organism with a certain structure, capable of functioning in a certain way, was a matter of pure chance, then the production of two similar organisms at more or less the same time had a vastly greater initial improbability. It is vastly less probable that I shall on two days running back a winner against which the odds are 100 to 1 than that I shall do it once. But it is not a question of two organisms, but millions! And an appeal to natural selection will not help you. The evolution must have taken place before natural selection could get to work. There have to be eyes with varying degrees of efficiency before the more efficient ones can be selected. The real problem is why there should be eyes at all.

The hypothesis of blind chance simply breaks down. Evolution is a matter of law. And if you will not have a teleological law—a law by which organisms are produced *in order that* they may see and hear and think, you must say that there is a blindly causal law by which organisms *had* to be produced who could see and hear and think. But did this law start to operate out of nothingness, by a pure chance?

Is a refusal to admit purpose in evolution based on a dispassionate study of the evidence, or is it a prejudice?

It must be admitted that the misuse by certain Christian apologists in the past of the "argument from design" to prove

137

the *goodness* of God may have helped to create the prejudice. The Christian faith in the goodness of God has quite other grounds, and we do not argue thus nowadays. But I believe the argument for purpose in or "behind" creation, based on our observation of the world around us and the living creatures in it, is absolutely sound.

12

THE GOD-MAN RELATION

Theism and Pantheism

It should not be necessary further to labour the point that what I am offering is a rational construction, and not a deductive argument, and that the same is true of *all* our beliefs about the real world. The following outline of the relation between the Divine awareness and ours, and its bearing on the identity of the Divine being with ours, does I submit, fit the facts "beautifully", and I can conceive of no other which does. On these grounds I feel the same sort of confidence that it is true that I feel whenever I am up against overwhelming circumstantial evidence. To begin with, let us revert to our earlier consideration of the criteria for truth which every finite rational being uses instinctively. We "demand", as we say, that reality shall be non-contradictory and, what is more, coherent or systematically unified. We regard the brute-factuality of mere juxtaposition, mere togetherness, as constituting as real a challenge to our reasoning powers as does apparent contradiction. This "demand" for connection, for system, forbids us to think of our thinking and the reality of which we think as two entirely separate realms. There must be some connection between the "structure" of our minds and that of reality. Our intellectual demands must therefore be more than demands; they must be insights. Since our most fundamental rational instinct is to seek to see reality as non-contradictory, as self-consistent, and also as completely systematic—as a unity—we must believe that reality *is* self-consistent and a systematic unity. That, in fact, is how we all *do* reason. We say that if the data before us contain contradictions, then in some degree they must be apparent and not real. And we equally feel that we have appearance and not complete reality when we are confronted by mere side-by-sideness, or by something which is a brute fact and which, for all we can see, need not have existed. We do not demand that reality *shall* be so-and-so. We say that reality *is* so-and-so, and that if what is before our minds does not comply, then it is, in those respects, appearance and not complete reality.

We must postulate, then, that the awareness of God is one which actually realizes the ideal which animates all our intellectual instincts. The rational instinct to seek consistency and unity, and to include ever more data—more facts—within the systematic unity, is, fundamentally, an instinct to expand our awareness to greater similarity with that of God. But we have postulated that exact similarity as between consciousnesses is complete identity. It follows that *if* a rational being *could* bring to completion the task which he sets himself of expanding his knowledge and systematizing it, he would *become* reality—become God. The task of increasing our "grasp" of truth and reality is not a process of copying something wholly external—it is a process of increasing union *with* reality. We need not be in the least shocked by this thought. It is not pantheistic; it is quite compatible with orthodox Christianity. The fact that a conditional sentence is true does not imply that the condition, in practice or even in principle, could be realized. It is true that if wishes were horses, beggars would ride, but a wish cannot, in the nature of things, turn itself into a horse without more ado. It is one thing, therefore, to say that the cognitive ideal which finite rational beings have ever before them could be realized only by their becoming God. It is quite another to say that they are on their way to becoming God. I affirm the first and deny the second.

What we can say, however, is that there is real identity between man and God, although the similarity-relation which is an identity-relation is one-sided. Everything in my awareness is included in God's but there are doubtless vast areas of experience in God which transcend *all* human awareness. An increase in experience and knowledge is an increased identity with God, but this does not prove that the process of increasing the identity-area is capable, even in principle, of being carried beyond definite limits. It is evident that there *are* such limits. We are capable, as rational beings, of seeing what the task is. But we can carry it out to a limited extent only. Physics, biology, and psychology, for example, have achieved considerable success in unifying their data. But the task of synthesising the sciences into One Science is quite beyond us. We cannot say that the thing cannot be done. Reality does, somehow, do it. But our intellects are incapable of seeing *how* it is done. We must admit our limitations.

Divine goodness

We have tried to analyse the Mystery of the God-man relation, and have seen that it is of such a nature that we must affirm both that the moral choices of self-conscious beings are free and that they are moments in a Divine purpose. But the question which clearly confronts us is whether there are sufficient grounds for our believing the Divine purpose to be good, in face of the existence of evil and pain. The answer I believe to be "Yes!".

First, we have seen reason to hold that God's awareness actually achieves that completely systematic unity which is the ideal of all human thinking. Now one of the outstanding characteristics of the good, as distinct from the bad, human life is that the former displays a unity which the latter lacks. It is unnecessary to argue this in detail here. It has been done again and again, since Plato first pointed out that the good life has a teleological unity, or is "harmonious"—the "lower" passions being duly subordinated to the "higher"—whereas the evil man is at war with himself. No modern thinker, of course, would claim that this is a complete account of the distinction between good and evil, but Plato was certainly calling attention to a very important characteristic of the good life. Goodness is undoubtedly associated in our minds with order, system and unity whereas the life of the bad man normally displays little teleological unity and often considerable inner conflict. The modern insistence of psychologists that the good and healthy human life is essentially an "integrated" life is further evidence in the same direction. We are, then, fully justified in regarding the Divine awareness, which by hypothesis is completely systematic and unified, as "good".

Secondly, we can appeal to our very deep conviction that when we describe certain actions as "right" or as "wrong", we are doing something more than merely expressing our emotions or taking up a practical attitude. I do not think that the issue between those modern philosophers who treat moral judgments as merely evincing subjective preferences or expressing emotions or attitudes, and those who, on the contrary, insist that they are statements about some objective fact, can be settled by a mere inspection or analysis, whether psychological or philosophical, of the judgments themselves. These judgments undoubtedly do express emotions and attitudes; there is no disagreement about that. But the question whether the widespread conviction of plain men that they do more than this—that they describe an objective situation—is to be regarded as a mistake, will be decided by wider meta-physical considerations. If one is committed to the meta-physical theory that objective reality consists only of imper-sonal entities or "forces", of electrons or pieces of matter or sensa or sensibilia, then one is bound to deny that moral judgments describe objective situations. Pieces of matter and sensa cannot have moral convictions so there is no objective standard with which to compare our moral judgments. But if we are right in insisting that objective reality is *more* ade-quately, although not, of course, completely adequately, described in terms of Mind and Will, then we shall quite con-sistently, indeed quite inevitably, regard our conviction that moral judgments are statements of objective reality as inspired in us by the immanent Mind. An action is right if it accords with the objective "Will" and wrong if it conflicts with it.

Thirdly, the argument of this book as a whole requires that it is not to the physical sciences but to human history that we shall look for a revelation in human terms of the nature of the transcendent God. And clearly the particular aspect of human history to which we must look is the history of man's religious convictions. There can be no question that the great masters of the spiritual life, the prophets and mystics, are unanimous in their insistence that the source of their religious experiences is God Himself, and that in them He is revealed as good.

If, then, the overruling Purpose is good, and if God's aware-ness—which is of course complete self-awareness—is of a complete systematic unity which is good, it follows that our statement that a man's awareness is completely included in that of God needs supplementing by the drawing of a dis-tinction between the *way* the good and the evil in the man are thus included.

Let us be clear as to the exact nature of the problem. We have insisted that the finite consciousnesses are included in the Divine consciousness. The use of the concept of inclusion is justified because we saw that as between non-spatial entities such as conscious beings exact similarity is exact identity. And we *needed* to insist that there is an area of identity between the finite and the Divine. For from the standpoint of Theism, God's omniscience must be maintained, and since complete knowledge of what a finite person is can be attained not by discursive or mediated knowledge but only by immediate "realization" or sympathetic similarity, i.e. identity, we are bound to maintain the *inclusion* of all finite awareness without subtraction in the Divine awareness. The ideal knowledge which all finite truth-seekers are implicitly seeking is—we saw good reason for believing—actually attained by God. But this ideal is nothing less than the ideal of complete, i.e. all-inclusive, as well as completely coherent or systematic realization. From *our* finite standpoint God is largely Other—is "outside"—for there are vast "areas" of *His* awareness which transcend *ours*. But we must believe that we do not confront Him as brute external facts, which He just *has* to accept. He sees us as part of the absolute unity of His Self-awareness.

Does this mean that our mistakes and our sins are included in the being of God and that therefore He makes mistakes and sins? Certainly not. Consider first the case of error. A good teacher can sympathize with the state of mind of the pupil who is making a mistake. Indeed, the question whether he *is* a good teacher turns very largely on his ability to put himself into the place of the pupil—to see *why* he is making just the mistake—to see that being in the state of mind he is in he is *bound* to make that mistake. And yet the teacher is fully aware that the mistake *is* a mistake and *why* it is. The teacher himself is free from that particular error not because he excludes it from his consciousness and sympathy but because he includes it in a special way, a special context. The

144

modern economist is free from the Luddites' error of seeing
the invention of machinery as a disaster in itself, but he is free
not by excluding it from his consciousness but including it
and seeing exactly *why* it is an error and why people such as
the Luddites were bound to see it as truth. His awareness
includes the judgment "The invention of machinery is a disaster", but it includes it in this special context. The judgment
"The invention of machinery is a disaster" exists both in (and
as therefore part of) the mind of the Luddite and in (and as
part of) the mind of the economist. But it is an error only as
it exists in the mind of the Luddite, for only there does it
exist in separation, exist without its proper context.

In a similar way we can see how we can, without identifying
sin with error, think of the awareness of God as including our
sins but being sinless. Sins, like errors, can be, so to speak
"cancelled" not merely by destruction but by supplementation. A good man, as distinct from an innocent child, can
"sympathize" fully with the state of mind of a sinner in yield-
ing to a temptation. Perfect goodness need not connote any
measure of ignorance—of lack of capacity for "entering
into" the state of mind of the sinner. But this does *not* involve
participation in the sin *as sin*.

The reader may—he probably will if the line I am taking is
unfamiliar to him—try to pick holes in my argument. But
let him beware—let him realize what he is doing. I expressly
stated that I was not going to attempt an "explanation" of
the unique relation between the Divine awareness and finite
awareness. Just because it is unique it cannot be *explained*,
in the sense of shown to be exactly similar to some other relation. True, I have used analogies—but only with the purpose
of showing that there is no positive reason for rejecting my
analysis of the Mystery as inherently unreasonable. My aim
in the last few pages has been to analyse the unique Mystery

of the relation between God and man as being such that:

1. We are free, or morally responsible beings.
2. The Universe is not an irrational chaos. We are not forced to use such terms as "irrationality" and "blind chance" in describing any feature of it.
3. Our freedom is compatible with God's omniscience.
4. We are ends in ourselves, and we can pursue ends which are ends in themselves, and yet God can "use" us, can take up our purposes into the unity of a larger Purpose, i.e. use us as ends to His means.
5. By Reality we mean the Universe as God sees it—and we must suppose His awareness to be complete self-awareness, free from potentiality, i.e. completely explicit and actual.
6. God must be conceived as "seeing" or "grasping" the Universe in such a way as to exclude all inconsistencies and incoherences and brute or external facts.
7. We are justified in postulating the absolute goodness of God, in spite of the existence of evil.

Divine grace

One very interesting result of our analysis is that it provides a rational background to that conviction of religious experience, characteristic of Christianity, that in our struggle against temptation our moral victories are due to Divine grace—we claim no credit for them—whereas our evil decisions are our own—we must accept responsibility for them. It is easy, of course, to see the superficial contradiction. At a first glance it would seem that if we are to be held responsible for our sins we should be credited with our good deeds. But it soon becomes apparent that there are difficulties here, for on such a view humility is hypocrisy. And Christian experience certainly rejects this superficial view, even at the cost of accepting an apparent contradiction. What I claim our analysis to have shown is that the Christian experience has, underlying it, a deeper rationality; the contradiction is seen to be apparent, not real. Let us examine this more closely.

When a human being makes a good moral decision his state of mind, his awareness, as we have called it, is included in and identical with the awareness of God. His decision can quite appropriately be called God acting in him, or, to use theological language, his action is by Divine grace. But, as we have seen, when he makes an evil choice, then the inclusion of his mental state in the Divine is an inclusion mediated by a special context. God realizes it, and in this sense includes it, but also knows that it flows from the evildoer's finitude— from the fact that as finite he *excludes* so much of the Divine life. God as it were accepts or includes the evil, but only within the context of His disapproval. In a very real sense, then, our evil choices are, by definition, ours and *not* God's, whereas our good ones are all of grace. At the cost of tedious repetition, let me emphasize that I am not offering this as a slick solution—least of all as a logically necessary or tauto-logical deduction. I am analysing something unique—a Mystery. I am saying that the unique nature of the God-man relation is such that we accept responsibility for our sins and attribute our moral victories to Divine grace. I am not attempt-ing to "explain" this, in the sense of showing that it is exactly analogous to some other phenomenon, for it is not, I am merely saying that we must recognize facts when we see them and use language appropriate to what we see.

Prayer

It is obvious that the account of the God-man relation which I have given is compatible with Christian experience of prayer. It clearly fits our experience of the value of *contemplative* prayer. And our insistence that all talk about the God-man relation—all talk, indeed, about reality which is metaphysically valid—must be conducted in personal language enables us to see the fallacy of certain popular criticisms of *petitionary* prayer. The notion that we cannot understand how God "answers" prayer unless we can show how prayer brings about its own answer "automatically", is seen to be merely silly. For that is to drop to the impersonal language-standpoint. Petitionary prayer is essentially an I-Thou transaction. There is no reason whatever for objecting to the statement that God "hears" (as we say) prayers, and answers them "if He thinks fit". Such language is, of course, anthropomorphic; it is adapted to our finite limitations. But it is far more appropriate than any form of language borrowed from mechanics—than any suggestion that prayer, as it were, pushes a button and brings a reaction.

Negative Statements about God

Before we come to our concluding chapter we ought to notice a point of some importance, namely that in speaking of the Divine awareness much of our language tends to be negative. Does this contradict our thesis that the Divine awareness must be thought of as absolutely actual and in no measure potential, and that it is all-inclusive. If it is all-inclusive, can we appropriately describe it in negative language?

The answer is that all our factual language is an expression of our positive belief—belief that the objective situation is positively characterized in a certain way. If the language is cast in negative form, this is merely a matter of linguistic convenience; it does not express a belief that reality can have negative characteristics; there *are* no negative characteristics. For example, if I say that the room was certainly not painted red I do not mean that the walls were covered with negative paint. I cast my statement in negative form because I cannot remember in exactly what colour it was painted but am sure the colour was one which, although as positive as red, was other than red. Red is incompatible with green, and green with red, but each is as positive as the other. Negative language expresses the vagueness or indefiniteness of our knowledge; it does not imply objective negative characteristics. The question whether we use negative or positive language is sometimes one on which we have a choice. We can say "not to the north" or "to the south". We can say "Not self-contradictory" or "self-consistent". But the existence of positive synonyms for negative expressions is more or less accidental; at any rate it is a matter of convenience. If there is no positive synonym in the dictionary for some particular negative expression, we can always coin one.

Now it is precisely because our knowledge of the awareness of God is vague and indefinite that we find it convenient to use negative terms. All Reality is what it *is*; and if we say it is not X, it is because we have positive, although vague knowledge that it must have some positive characteristic which excludes X. We say that God, the Reality-awareness, *cannot* be confronted with mystery, for by definition God knows the world as it really is, and the term 'mystery' connotes subjective ignorance, not objective quality. He *cannot* be confronted, as we are, by "external" or "brute" facts; the world does *not* oppose His Will as it does ours. All this is expressed in negative terms. But in this negative way we are trying to express positive characteristics. God's awareness includes all ours and removes the element of ignorance and vagueness by supplementation, not cancellation.

13

THE MYSTERY OF EVIL;
CHRISTIAN DUALISM

The most fundamental difference between on the one hand, the greatest truth about Reality that human awareness can attain and, on the other hand, reality-awareness or God's awareness, consists in the fact that man's awareness is conditioned by those forms of time and space which God's awareness transcends. To see that this is so is to hold the key to the solution—so far as the human mind *can* achieve a solution—of the profoundest problem in the philosophy of religion—the problem of evil and suffering.

The human mind can transcend the time process in the sense that it can know that reality-awareness *must* transcend it. This is an instance of the fact that the human mind can, in a sense, transcend its own limitations. The animal's mind not only is limited, but it can *in no wise* transcend its limitations; for it does not know it *has* limitations. But man does realize his limitations; he can see in what ways he is limited; and in a very real sense he therefore transcends his limitations. But this transcendence is bare and abstract. All our detailed, concrete statements about the Universe are in the time form, and therefore essentially anthropomorphic.

We can summarize the whole case for affirming that God's

awareness is not, as ours is, an awareness in the time form by pointing out that the finite mind cannot contemplate any infinite regress such as that of time, or of Euclidian space, without a sense of mystery. Now a sense of mystery is, in the nature of things, subjective. Nothing can be intrinsically or objectively mysterious. Our sense of mystery, indeed, is accompanied by a conviction that what we are contemplating cannot *really* be what it *appears* to be. Now since we define Reality as "the Whole as God knows it", it follows that there can be no element of mystery in the Divine awareness.

It is interesting, although not, perhaps, important, to consider whether our sense of mystery can always be analysed into an awareness of contradiction. We might deny this, and say that our awareness of any infinite regress, such as a time or space with no beginning or ending, no limits, is accompanied by a feeling of frustration, of being given an endless task—a feeling indeed which at times can be frightening, and that this is independent of any awareness of contradiction. And clearly God cannot be conceived as being confronted with baffling mysteries; there is by definition nothing, there is no one, "outside" Him to confront Him with brute facts of any sort, let alone set Him tasks beyond Him. But on the other hand it could be argued that there is an *implicit* awareness of contradiction in our contemplation of infinite series. For it can be maintained that reality must be definite—must be precisely what it is, and that an infinite series of durations or successions is indefinite. We are therefore contemplating something which is both definite and indefinite; we have reduced our mystery to a contradiction; we therefore dismiss infinite regresses as only apparent and not real.

In the case of the time regress there is a further element of mystery. For us finite beings, the past, is, as we say, "gone for ever". It has just vanished into nothingness. And the future, too, is not existent. Both past and future are sheer nothingness; they just "are not". Only the momentary present is "real", in the sense of *actual*. Now rational beings cannot believe that in looking at the objective situation in this way we are seeing it "as it really is". We just *cannot* accept as a simple and accurate statement of objective fact that a non-existent future is for ever turning itself into a momentarily existent present and then vanishing again into non-existent past. Our rational revolt against this conception is no arbitrary fad. We awake to existence and find ourselves equipped with this reason which revolts. If we are wise we shall regard this rational instinct as being as truly a clue to reality as is the stream of sense-data. In some sense the past and the future *must* be real. God's awareness *must* include an awareness of both.

Now it is impossible to exaggerate the importance of the fact that *all* our statements about reality, *whether true or false*, are conditioned by our finite time-awareness. Let us ask ourselves how this is relevant to the so-called problem of reconciling belief in the goodness of God with the facts of evil and pain.

In Chapter 12 I outlined our reasons for ascribing goodness to God. But how can this goodness be revealed to beings who experience time as we experience it? How can Divine goodness be revealed in the evolutionary process and in the drama of human life? Clearly only by the revelation of a good *purpose*; we must be able to see God as working in time towards good ends. We must, that is, think of Him as achieving them *gradually*—as "willing" or as "working towards" good results. His infinitude is seen as *omnipotence*—as a potency which actualizes itself only gradually. *If it actualized itself in a flash there would be no time process.* If, therefore, we are to see God in history at all we must see Him as opposed, hindered, thwarted—and therefore as suffering.

Our finite time-form awareness is not, as a whole, erroneous. The distinction of truth from error is one which breaks out *within* the field of human awareness. There are true and there are false human judgments; one cannot characterize the whole field of human awareness as illusory. Humanly speaking, we must say that God "intends" us to think under the forms of time and space, with all that this involves. Indeed, just because God is, for and in Himself, unlimited and all-knowing, His awareness includes, although it transcends, time and space awareness.

The revelation of goodness in time, then, is *essentially* the revelation of a dualism. The *essence* of goodness, as a time phenomenon, is its conflict with evil. A "goodness" without such a conflict would be not goodness but innocence. Human beings could not be good unless they encountered evil. The good will, in man and in God, is essentially a will which freely rejects and opposes evil. And such a dualism clearly involves suffering—in man and in God. Men, of course, do not always choose good, and, as we have seen, they must accept responsibility for their evil decisions. But in Chapter 12 we saw a threefold reason for ascribing goodness to God—the complete unity or integration of the Divine awareness, the moral consciousness of man, and the insight of prophet, mystic and saint. While therefore we must insist that the time process is essentially a dualism—a fight between good and evil—we are not left with a *final*, an *absolute*, dualism. The fight is real, the pain involved is real, but from the Divine standpoint which transcends our time awareness the conflict is eternally won. This justifies us in using such metaphors as "God is *in control*".

But while we must not say that the dualism is ultimate, the simple fact is that it is only God who can, so to speak, be

153

a monist, and we are quite incapable of seeing reality from His monistic standpoint. We are creatures of time and space, and the philosophy of the Christian religion must, on the whole, be dualistic. It is far wiser to accept the dualism than to attempt facile reconciliations or to offer spurious solutions of the problem of evil and pain. It is one thing to say, as I have said, that the human mind is capable of seeing that in some sense real goodness presupposes real evil—capable, that is, of seeing how shallow is the argument that a good God would necessarily "make" a world free from pain and evil. It is quite another to claim that we can see *how* every evil feature of life is taken up into a larger good. While on the one hand the Christian must never admit that the problem of evil is *intrinsically* insoluble—must never admit that the existence of evil and pain is inconsistent with our ascription of goodness to God, yet on the other hand we cannot know *how* the final synthesis or reconciliation or unity is attained. And above all we must not claim that some particular evil and suffering which appears to us quite purposeless and pointless is disguised good. When a child catches poliomyelitis we must not say that it is "all for the best", or that we must submit to God's will. God's will is revealed in our efforts to *oppose* the disease, to kill the bacteria; the disease itself is *opposing* God's will.

And if we are asked: "Why, then, did God make the evil spirits or the chaotic or lawless forces which oppose Him?" The best answer, as the preceding discussion has shown, is to disallow the question. The whole conception of God as "making" finite creatures is false. We have to use a different metaphysical model or directive. We have to say that God is truly "revealed" by good and distorted by evil, lawlessness and chaos. Such an answer will not be convincing to a person whose mind has not been prepared by a careful study of the considerations which I have urged in this book, but that is no objection to the answer. No really important human question can be answered fully in a couple of sentences which would be immediately intelligible and convincing to the unreflective mind. There are many questions which might be asked of a mathematician, a physicist or a biologist to which a perfectly reasonable, and indeed the only possible, answer would be that the questioner will be able to understand the answer only if he is prepared to spend time and patience in grasping some fundamental concepts. Why, then, should it be thought that there is something suspect about an answer to a question in the sphere of philosophy or theology if its force cannot be immediately perceived by Tom, Dick or Harry? It may be replied that religion is *intended* for Tom, Dick and Harry, but that does not affect the point at issue. Tom can have faith and can live a religious life without analysing or questioning his intuitions. But one cannot have it both ways. One should not raise intellectual questions about one's faith unless one is prepared to submit to the discipline necessary to answer them adequately. One should not raise difficult questions and expect easy answers.

To summarize. Logic demands that beings who experience reality under the form of time and succession must *inevitably* picture God as having "purposes"; His infinitude *must* be seen as an omnipotence which actualizes itself gradually; His goodness *must* be seen as suffering because His purposes are seen as opposed and even thwarted. I am very far from suggesting that this purely logical approach is sufficient for religion. It gives us but the skeleton of a living faith; revelation and religious experience must clothe it with flesh and blood. But it would be foolish to disparage skeletons. The value of our insight into the logical implications of our time-awareness lies in its rejection of the old anti-Christian contention that

God cannot be thought of as both good and omnipotent—that He could be either one or the other but not both. We see good and evil as dialectical; they are thesis and antithesis; and we have seen sound reasons for holding that it is of the essence of finitude to see reality thus, and that the final synthesis is attainable only by a Mind which knows the Whole in complete systematic unity.

Our analysis should make us beware of short and easy justifications of the ways of God to men. In popular Christian apologetics it is often said that God does not "send" evil but that He "permits" it. This is an instance of the use, and the possibility of the abuse, of a metaphysical model. On page 12 I quoted Dr. Mace as saying of certain models that "not one of them is entirely absurd. Each draws attention to something of interest and importance. Absurdity results when some irrelevant features of the model are attributed to whatever is modelled." Now the model—or the "myth" if you like—of God "permitting" evil may be tolerated as a concrete picture of the abstract truth that reality is systematic and not chaotic, and that from the Divine standpoint evil is transcended by supplementation. But the objection to it, the danger in it, is that almost inevitably the unreflective mind will introduce an irrelevant feature of the model—will take it too literally, too anthropomorphically. There will be a picture of God up in the sky looking down and saying: "I think I shall let little Sarah Jones get poliomyelitis!" A God who is revealed in the time process by His *opposition* to evil is better not described as *permitting* it. It only makes for confusion in the popular mind. A working clergyman, in the business of visiting parishioners in their sorrows, is far nearer the ultimate truth if he frankly says that the evil is *not* the will of God. In the phenomenon of poliomyelitis, the Divine mind is revealed in man's attempt to *exterminate* the bacteria. One cannot have a consistent human picture of someone both exterminating a germ and "creating" or "permitting" it. Reality, for us human beings, is most truly pictured as the strife of a good God against evil, in which process He, like us, and with us, is hurt.

Christian Theology, then, dealing as it does with our time-awareness of Reality and not with Reality-awareness in and for itself, must be frankly dualistic. Now this, it seems to me, is implicit in the Christian doctrine of the Divine Son or Christ—the Second Person in the Trinity. And here, curiously enough, I join with Barth, to whom the rational approach I have advocated is anathema. We cannot say anything detailed and particular about God except as God is revealed in the time-process, revealed as "God the Son". I do not agree, and indeed the whole argument of this book is directed against the view, that our intellects are incapable of any valid arguments for the existence of God and that rational theology is impossible. We can, as we have seen, make significant and valid judgments about certain general characteristics of the Divine experience. But whenever we make any detailed statement about what God was or is doing or suffering in the time process, we are talking about God the Son. Practically, that is to say religiously, we are concerned only with God the Son —God as revealed to man in the conceptual form which the human mind can understand.

But does this mean that statements about God the Son are not objectively true—are not statements about God's *actual* being or experience but only about how He *appears* to us? Does it mean that God is not really acting, nor really experiencing a time process, not really being opposed and therefore not really suffering, but that that is merely how He appears, and is bound to appear, to us? Certainly not. For we have seen that precisely because God's awareness is all-inclusive it *includes* our time-awareness. True, our time-awareness is transcended in the absolute self-awareness of God the Father, but it is transcended not by cancellation but by supplementation. This is the justification for the Christian belief that what is in popular language called the "creation" of the world and finite beings is through the medium of a Logos—for the belief that the existence of finite beings implies an objective differentiation in God Himself. God is not an abstract unity —a pure being which is pure nothing—but a concrete unity of differences. God's awareness includes *all* the particular time-awareness of finite beings and includes therefore a *universal* time-awareness—a Logos. There is humanity in God, and because of this, Divinity can be manifested in man.

God's transcendence of our time-awareness is by supplementation, and therefore He experiences the qualities which our finite experiences possess in virtue of their very *exclusion* of the rest of the Divine awareness. God fully realizes our very subjectivity, our sense of being units in some sense "separate" from Him. Here I must remind the reader that we are not making a logically necessary deduction from self-evident propositions, nor are we attempting the absurd task of "explaining" what is unique by showing that it is like something else. All that we are called upon to do, all that in the nature of things we can do, is to analyse the mystery of the absolutely unique God-man relation—to find the ultimate language in which human beings can describe it.

When, then, the Christian is challenged to justify the ways of God to man, he has a right to ask from what standpoint the discussion is to be conducted—whether in language which presupposes the time series as practically "real" in the popular sense of the word, or from the standpoint of an ultimate metaphysical construction in which time is seen, in the purely technical sense explained on page 51 to be "unreal". Now there is every reason to suppose that from the Divine standpoint the answer to many of our human questions involves the transformation of the questions themselves. We ourselves sometimes feel a difficulty in answering the questions of very small children because we feel that there just is no answer to the question in the form in which the child asks it. He has to wait until he is old enough to arrive at a standpoint from which he ceases to ask the question in that form. In the study of philosophy we frequently have to criticize the questions themselves, and sometimes when we have finished our criticism, there is no question left to be answered. The question of "justifying the ways of God to men" is a question of this type. That the question of reconciling the existence of good and the existence of evil achieves a *formally* complete solution in the Divine awareness is certain. There are no contradictions in reality. But how it is done we cannot know.

The question, then, must be discussed from the standpoint of our human time-awareness. Indeed, it *arises* from that standpoint. Now from this standpoint language about God is language about the Spirit immanent in all good men and women in their struggle with evil, and feeling all the vicarious suffering involved in the struggle. The Eternal Son, indwelling human beings as the Holy Spirit, does not need "justification". He did not "create" and He does not "permit" evil. He is eternally fighting it. The answer to the problem of justifying the ways of God to men is to point to the essentially dualistic nature of Christian theology. The Universe, for us, is essentially a struggle between good and evil. We have to use metaphors. The good "reveals", the evil "distorts", that Reality which is the Divine awareness. The good is "nearer to the heart" of Reality than the evil. We can leave it there. We have seen abundant rational justification for this faith,

159

but this is not, of course, to say that men normally arrive at it by reasoning.

As this book is a study of rational theology, of the philosophical basis of Christian theology, and is not a theological treatise, it would be beyond its scope to discuss the Christian doctrine that the Eternal Son was uniquely incarnate in Jesus Christ. But it is a simple fact of history, and not mere theory, that because of the life and death of Jesus and the events following, including the religious experiences of Paul and of the author of the Fourth Gospel, men became *conscious* of the extraordinary nature of the God-man relation which we have been considering. It was because of what happened in Palestine nineteen centuries ago that men became aware of the point of identity between God and man—of the humanity in God and the Divinity in man. Some of the ancient Greeks sneered at the human tendency to imagine God in man's image. But the Hebrews had had deeper insight, or a clearer Revelation. They had seen the one sufficient justification for imagining God in man's image—that He had made man in *His* image. But this talk of images is metaphor. The rational implication is *identity*—identity in difference, as we have seen. And the rational implications were actually wrought out in history. Had they not been, no rational theologian would have existed in the twentieth century to write a book like this.

INDEX

161